Assessment Guidelines for Sign Language Interpreting

Training Programmes

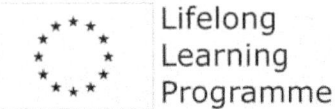
Lifelong Learning Programme

This project has been funded with support from the European Commission. This publication reflects the views only of the author, and the Commission cannot be held responsible for any use which may be made of the information contained therein.

ISBN: 9789081306560

© European Forum of Sign Language Interpreters, 2013

Edited by: efsli

Cover design by: Livii Hollman

Cover photos: efsli. efsli working seminars: Utrecht (November 2011), Hamburg (March 2012) and Dublin (February 2013)

Authors: Lorraine Leeson, Lourdes Calle Alberdi, Sarah Bown

Printed by: Print House, Madrid, Spain

No part of this publication may be produced, stored in a retrieval system or transmitted in any form or any means (electronic, photocopying, recording or otherwise), without the prior written permission of the publisher.

Whenever you publish an article/paper or present results based on or referring to the efsli learning outcomes data, please include the following acknowledgement or an appropriate equivalent:

"We wish to thank the European Forum of Sign Language Interpreters (efsli) for providing the data used in this paper. The European Forum of Sign Language Interpreters (efsli) is a not-for-profit ONG representing sign language interpreters across Europe – www.efsli.org"

The European Forum of Sign Language Interpreters (efsli) is a not-for-profit NGO consisting of national associations of sign language interpreters. It is the only organisation representing sign language interpreters at a European level, comprising a very wide network of sign language interpreters and organisations. efsli fosters a vision of high European-wide standards of sign language interpreting services which enable interpreters to fulfill their work in a professional manner.

Being a forum where good practices and expertise are shared between all stakeholders in the field of sign language interpreting, efsli aims to constantly enhance the status of the profession through higher standards of continuing education, professional recognition and adequate working conditions.

The present publication is an example of efsli's contribution to defining this process of quality improvement.

Table of Contents

1. Foreword	6
2. Acknowledgments	7
3. Prologue	8
4. General assessment recommendations	11
4.1 The purpose of assessment	12
4.2 Threshold academic standards	14
4.3 The testing cycle	14
4.4 Assessment within interpreter training programmes	19
5. Assessment	21
5.1 Written texts assessment	21
5.2 Language tests	23
5.3 Interpreting tests	25
5.4 Interpreting portfolio	29
5.5 Placement learning	33
6. Glossary	38
7. References	43
Appendix 1: Further resources	47
Appendix 2: Sample matrices and semi scripted role play	51

1. Foreword

Peter Llewellyn-Jones, efsli president

This document, together with its sister publication, *Learning Outcomes for Graduates of a Three Year Sign Language Interpreting Training Programme*, is the result of a consultation process that involved more than a hundred interpreters and interpreter educators across Europe together with further input from efsli's Committee of Experts. They present the minimum standards required of a competent interpreter in, we hope, a form that can be adapted to suit the types and levels of training provision across the member states.

They are, obviously, just the beginning of a process; not the end. They will need to be reviewed and updated regularly in the years ahead as Deaf people across Europe gain access to ever widening social and employment opportunities. Technological advances are likely to have an increasing impact on the work of interpreter and, as formalised training develops, so too will our understanding of best practice in teaching and assessment.

2. Acknowledgements

The efsli team

efsli is very grateful to all those who contributed to the planning, writing and preparation of these Assessment Guidelines. Our particular thanks go to all the interpreters and interpreter trainers from across Europe who participated in the efsli Working Seminars in Utrecht, Hamburg and Dublin and the members of the efsli Committee of Experts who commented on and contributed to the drafts (see below).

Special thanks are due to Lourdes Calle Alberdi for coordinating the project and preparing the initial drafts and to Lorraine Leeson and Sarah Bown who spent countless hours producing the final version. Thanks also to Liivi Hollman for providing the necessary continuity to complete the project.

We would particularly like to thank the institutions who shared sample matrices with us (Appendix 2), namely, the University of Wolverhampton (United Kingdom), Trinity College Dublin (Ireland) and Macquarie University (Sydney, Australia)

The members of the efsli Committee of Experts during this process were:
- Sarah Bown
- Barry Allan Davey
- Ebru Diriker
- Zane Hemma
- Robert G. Lee
- Lorraine Leeson (Chair)
- Peter Llewellyn-Jones
- Christian Rathmann
- Camilla Warnicke

3. Prologue

Lorraine Leeson and Sarah Bown, efsli Committee of Experts (eCE)

"We plan. We develop. We deliver. We assess and evaluate the results of the assessment. We revise, deliver the revised material, and assess and evaluate again. Perfection is always just out of reach; but continually striving for perfection contributes to keeping both our instruction fresh and our interest in teaching piqued."

(E.S. Grassian)

Assessment is critically important to the work that we do in the education and preparation of sign language interpreters. It is also an area that has not been widely researched or discussed in the literature within the domain of sign language interpreter education. In light of these key factors, a collaborative pan-European discussion amongst interpreter educators and practitioners from 16 countries led to the development of these *Assessment Guidelines for European Sign language Interpreting Training Programmes* at the *III efsli working seminar: Quality Assessment - a European Model for Sign Language Interpreter Education and Training*, held in Dublin (Ireland) in February 2013. The aim of this working seminar was to revise the efsli *Learning Outcomes for Graduates of a Three Year Interpreting Programme* draft, provide feedback on the document before completing the definitive version, and consider how the learning outcomes under consideration might be assessed. The proposals gathered in the Dublin workshops were revised and completed afterwards by the efsli project coordinator, Lourdes Calle Alberdi, and the efsli Committee of Experts (eCE), chaired by Lorraine Leeson. The final outcome of this process is the present document which accompanies the efsli *Learning Outcomes for Graduates of a Three Year Sign Language Interpreting Programme*, which will be presented to the European Parliament in winter 2013.

The purpose of this document is to present a set of possible types of assessment which are in use throughout Europe when assessing learning outcomes within educational programmes. The efsli *Learning Outcomes for Graduates of a Three Year Sign Language Interpreting Programme,* served as a basis for the discussion in the Dublin workshops and provided the point of reference for the present guidelines. However, while these guidelines are pitched at a three-year undergraduate course, it is our hope that this document will also function as a point of reference and resource to those who may be working outside of that framework.

prologue

The delivery of interpreter education across Europe is diverse. In creating this document, we were highly aware of the diversity of the more than 65 training programmes for sign language interpreters across Europe (De Wit 2012). Programme length, structures, regulations, along with human and financial resources differ greatly from place to place but we note that in terms of language pairs, there are at least four interpreting & translation pathways that can be delivered in an inclusive training programme:

- Working between a national/regional sign language and the national/regional spoken language

- Working between a national/regional sign language and the national/regional written language

- Working between two signed languages

- Working between a national/regional signed language and International Sign

We emphasise that this document is presented as a consensus document, a document of reference. It is not meant to be prescriptive in any shape or form. We emphasise this because we wish to ensure that readers bear in mind that learning outcomes can be assessed in several ways – there is more than one 'correct' way to approach assessment, and often approaches to assessment will be guided by why we are assessing at a particular point in a course or programme, and what resources we have to work with.

We also emphasise that we are not saying that every learning outcome that is included in the efsli *Learning Outcomes for Graduates of a Three Year Sign Language Interpreting Programme* must be assessed via a separate assessment: best practice assessment procedures will find ways to include the assessment of several learning outcomes within one assessment type.

With the pan-European Bologna Process leading to the harmonisation of European Union higher education, the publication of learning outcomes and assessment data has come to be expected across European institutions of higher education, where an increasing number of sign language interpreter training programmes are housed. The kinds of assessment that take place within higher education are varied, ranging from traditional written exams to portfolio building and including live examina-

prologue

tions for candidates in the practice professions like physiotherapy, nursing, medicine, for example. The focus we take in this document is on the formative and summative assessment of students across the life of their undergraduate education in the field of interpreting.

This document is divided into two parts; general recommendations and specific assessment tools. A glossary of terms has also been included to provide definitions of core terminology used.

Angelelli and Jacobson (2009: 3-4) wrote that "assessments seem to be conducted in a vacuum, and the processes involved need to be accurately described in order to ensure transparency". In a bid to move towards a position of greater transparency in the assessment of sign language interpreters, we have also included some sample rubrics from programmes that have been evaluated by quality control authorities and external examination processes that we hope may stimulate further sharing in line with the tradition of efsli trainers.

We encourage readers to refer to the following website for information about quality assurance in higher education across Europe, though we note that not all countries that have established regulatory bodies are included in the listings. (www.qrossroads.eu/quality-assurance-and-accreditation, accessed October 2013).

As a final suggestion, we propose that this document is a starting point, not an endpoint: we envisage that as with any assessment cycle, discussion around best practice assessment of sign language interpreters will require revisiting on a regular basis, not least arising because of rapid technological changes which impact on the norms of practice in our profession, for example, the development and roll out of remote interpreting, video relay interpreting, as well as the increasing availability of online and blended learning opportunities.

Lorraine Leeson and Sarah Bown
On behalf of the efsli Committee of Experts
October 2013

4. General assessment recommendations

"Everything that can be counted does not necessarily count; everything that counts cannot necessarily be counted"

Albert Einstein

The issue of assessment of interpreters, of both spoken and signed languages, is one which demands further attention, both in terms of research and in the sharing of information about methods of assessment, test protocols and outcomes (Salaets and Vermeerbergen 2011, Pochhacker 2004, Angelelli and Jacobson 2009, Leeson 2011). Leeson notes that "the assessment of signed language interpreters is fraught with concern about fitness to practice, the competencies required to interpret effectively in a broad range of settings, idealized notions of desired competence versus minimal skill levels required to undertake the task at hand, as well as issues relating to language teaching, language status, and societal attitudes toward deaf communities and signed languages." (ibid: 153) These are key issues that efsli trainers discussed, and which this document addresses in what is the first attempt to bring together the collective experience and insights of interpreter educators from across Europe on the issue of formative and summative assessment of candidates for the sign language interpreting profession.

In considering assessment, a number of key component issues need to be addressed. These include:

- The purpose of assessment

- The idea of threshold academic standards

- The fundamental principles of assessment (validity, reliability, fairness, transparency)

- The testing cycle

general assessment recommendations

4.1 The purpose of assessment

"No test can be a substitute for proper training, nor is testing per se a remedy for a lack of interpreters. Tests do not produce interpreters; proper education does"

(Niska 1999: 278)

While assessment is an essential component of evaluating student progress, we also need to see it as an integral part of the learning process. In this way, we can see that formative and summative learning can assist students as they learn as well as serving as tools for educators and key stakeholders.

As the British Quality Assurance Agency for Higher Education (QAA) notes, "For the student, individual pieces of assessment may provide a source of motivation for study; they promote learning by providing feedback (or "feedforward", emphasizing the learning focus of feedback) on performance and help students to identify their strengths and weaknesses. For the lecturer, assessment provides an opportunity to evaluate the knowledge, understanding, ability and skills attained by different students. The overall profile of student performance offers useful information for assessing the effectiveness of course content and teaching methods, thereby facilitating improvement. For the institution, assessment provides information upon which decisions as to students' progression and the receipt of awards may be based. The assessment process enables the institution to ensure that appropriate standards are being met, in accordance with nationally agreed frameworks, such as subject benchmark statements and the frameworks for higher education qualifications. Information generated by assessment, such as mark or grade distributions, forms a valuable tool for quality assurance and enhancement." (ibid: 4).

Thus, the purpose of testing is a critical factor in determining what kind of test should be applied in any given setting (i.e. a written exam of knowledge, a performance test, etc.). Test purpose is typically associated with the distinction between achievement tests and proficiency tests. Achievement tests are associated with the process of instruction. They assess what a student has achieved vis-à-vis the curriculum taught on a programme. McNamara (2000) reports that achievement measures tend to be associated with portfolio-based assessments, course tests, as well as the assessment of course work. On the other hand, achievement tests focus on student development with respect to course learning outcomes. Achievement testing has a number of key criteria: (1) it should support the teaching it relates to; (2) it may be self-enclosed (that is, may focus on aspects of language grammar or use that has been covered in the curriculum rather than focusing on language use in the wider world); (3) it can be highly innovative, and is often associated with "alternative assessment", which stresses that assessment is integrated with the goals of the curriculum, and pushes for a constructive relationship between teaching and learning (following McNamara 2000).

While achievement tests look back at skill development in an individual student with respect to what they have already learned, proficiency tests are concerned with future use, without reference to the teaching process. Such future skill use is considered as the criterion against which proficiency is measured. *Performance features* are frequently incorporated into the design of proficiency testing. For example, aspects of the linguistic environment that medical personnel will encounter are included as test criterion (i.e., can a doctor communicate effectively with a patient who speaks language X?) (Leeson 2011).

Other terms that are frequently used in the literature on testing include formative and summative assessment. Formative assessment has a developmental purpose and is designed to help learners learn more effectively by giving them feedback on their performance and on how it can be improved and/or maintained. Reflective practice by students sometimes contributes to formative assessment (e.g. self-critiques of interpreting or language performance, a reflective diary, but critically, this is the case only when feedback is provided) (QAA 2012). Summative assessment indicates the extent of a learner's success in meeting the assessment criteria used to gauge the intended learning outcomes of a module or programme. Another way of expressing this distinction is that in summative assessment, the marks awarded for the assessment count towards the final mark of the module/ programme/award. In some countries, for some professions, summative assessment links to professional registration, and thus is critically important as a stepping stone into professional life (QAA 2012). Even where no professional statutory registration process exists yet, we can recognize the significance of summative assessment as a mechanism for establishing that a candidate is fit to practice at entry level in the profession before graduating from a programme of study.

Thus, we can see that the purpose of testing is a critically important element underpinning decisions about how to test and what to test at what point in a student's career.

general assessment recommendations

4.2 Threshold academic standards

Fitness to practice norms can also be described with respect to the idea of threshold academic standards. These are the minimum acceptable level of achievement that a student has to demonstrate to be eligible for an academic award. As the British QAA points out, for equivalent awards, the threshold level of achievement should be the same across a member state. However, individual awarding bodies are responsible for setting the grades, marks or classification that differentiate between levels of student achievement above the threshold academic standard within an individual award (after QAA 2012: 3).

4.3 The testing cycle

Test design involves 3 key phases: (1) Consideration of background issues, (2) Test content and test method design, and (3) Review, validation and revision. Background issues are those that influence test method and design, such as consideration of the constraints that impact on test design and implementation as well as the resources (financial, physical, human) that are available for test development and operation. As McNamara (2000: 29) notes, "As assessment becomes more authentic, it also becomes more expensive, complex and potentially unwieldy". Given that most programmes operate with limited resources, creativity is a key factor for successful assessment. One possibility is that interpreting departments work in tandem with other departments in their institution which may allow for input into assessments like role-plays. For example, colleagues or postgraduate students from a medical department might participate in the preparation and roll-out of medical interpreting role-plays.

New technologies are increasingly present in educational settings, and can be harnessed for assessment purposes, for example, portfolio building. The creation of online forums to facilitate discussion in relation to a given topic can provide an opportunity for reflection and debate with reference to the interpreting literature. Such approaches are becoming commonplace with the increased roll-out of online or blended learning.

Once the decision has been made regarding which assessment type will best evaluate which learning outcomes, another critical component for consideration is test security. Factors that need to be decided in advance include whether the test content is unseen by candidates or should be partially shared. Should topics in interpreting exams be known or unknown in advance? There are legitimate rationales for all options, and assessment planners must consider these and be able to explicitly state why a certain type of test was selected at a certain threshold level. Finally, external factors such as examination protocols within the institution that must be followed, assessment bodies who have agreed on specific formats for testing and reporting back or for accreditation of programmes must be considered and factored into the assessment process.

In implementing a test cycle, a new test is ideally trialled in advance of implementation in order to ensure that the set of "rules" for the test, comprising written instructions for implementation are workable. Before this happens, design decisions regarding the test must be made. These must explicate the test's structure, duration, authenticity, source of testing material, the extent to which authentic materials are altered, response format, test rubric, and scoring system. Test materials are then written to these specifications, trialled, and potentially, revised before a cohort of students take them for the first time. At the same time, it is acknowledged that due to constraints on time, resources and sample populations, this can be difficult to do. However, this cycle is worthwhile in terms of solidifying the validity of the test process (Leeson 2011). A mechanism for supporting test validity is ensuring that 'mock' examination content is made available to students and ensuring that students have access to the test specifications prior to the test. Such approaches are hallmarks of university education and are also applied in many 'high stakes' testing domains (e.g., in Canada, AVLIC make sample tests available to candidates who will take their national registration test) (Leeson 2011).

The British Quality Assurance Agency's document, "Understanding Assessment: its role in safeguarding academic standards and quality in higher education. A guide for early career staff" (2012: 8) includes some helpful sample questions that may assist when preparing assessments for sign language interpreters:

- Does the assessment process enable learners to demonstrate achievement of all the intended learning outcomes?
- Are there criteria that enable internal and external examiners to distinguish between different categories of achievement?
- Can there be full confidence in the security and integrity of assessment procedures?
- Does the assessment strategy have an adequate formative function in developing

general assessment recommendations

student abilities?

- What evidence is there that the standards achieved by learners meet the minimum expectations for the award, as measured against relevant subject benchmark statements and the qualifications framework?

They suggest that the development of a grid which indicates how assessment methods map onto stated learning outcomes can be a helpful mechanism although they warn that this by itself may not demonstrate the appropriateness or otherwise of the method of assessment applied. Working with such a grid is also a useful tool that allows educators an overview of their programmatic assessment model to prevent 'over assessment' or duplication/unevenness of assessment type, e.g. bunching up, and to balance out an uneven spread .

In terms of selecting methods of assessment, they suggest the following general principles for consideration (ibid: 8):

- The preference for using more than one assessment method (unless there is a compelling reason to use only one)

- The need to ensure that students have opportunities for formative assessment in a method that is being experienced for the first time in the programme.

Another factor that demands consideration is that of accommodations and adjustments required to support students with disabilities who present for evaluation in line with European and national laws that address equality of access. While we are conscious that this document focuses only on the issue of providing guidelines for assessment, the issue of equality extends to the whole student life cycle . We refer readers to Section 3 of the QAA document on disability (2010).

Fairness is a key principle in assessment and this requires transparency around what is being tested at what stages of progress and what happens if a student fails to meet the requirements at any stage of the programme. The QAA (ibid: 15) lists the following as some of the issues that must be considered when approaching marking:

- A marking scale (we have included some samples in Appendix 2)

- Marking schemes (often called "grade descriptors")

- Whether anonymous marking is required (e.g. for written examinations);

- Various forms of second marking and the role of the external examiner(s) (sometimes referred to as 'moderation')

- Using quantitative data (e.g. grades across cohorts, across time frames)

- Administrative procedures for recording and verifying marks.

As we note later, the issue of transparency and fairness is one of critical importance when considering work placements where it is simply not possible to ensure that all students have access to the same range of learning experiences. Further, if assessments were to take place in the placement setting, the issue of consistency across assessment for all candidates must be given due regard. This extends to the issue of who the raters are and what training and teaching qualifications they have received to prepare them for their task. The issue of inter-rater reliability and intra-rater reliability are other key links in the chain of assessment. We also refer the reader to Sawyer (2004: 101-2) who we paraphrase here in summing up questions that we need to ask about the reliability of the assessments we stand over:

- Is the score consistent when different graders mark the same work from the same student? (inter-rater reliability)

- If the same rater judges the same work on different occasions, is their marking consistent? (intra-rater reliability)

- Is the score consistent when the same test is taken at different times in different places by the same examinee? (test-retest reliability)

- Is the score consistent when similar versions of the same exam are taken by similar populations? (parallel forms)

Fairness also extends to ensuring that pathways to a qualification entail assessments designed to capture the key competencies for practice that have been set down by national qualifications authorities and other relevant regulatory bodies (e.g. statutory or non-statutory licensing bodies). Given this, it is useful to consider Bown's (2013) consideration of the six main employability criteria that British employers argue "can transform organisations and add value early in their [graduates] careers" (HEA, 2006, p. 140), namely cognitive skills/brainpower, generic competencies/personal capabilities, technical ability, business and/or organization awareness, and practical elements such as vocational courses. Bown and Dekesel (2009, 2010, 2011) argue that building from these descriptions, at least 15 employability

general assessment recommendations

skills can be extrapolated that could be seen as containing reflective components. Bown (2013: 52) lists these as including:

- The ability to participate in and review quality control processes
- To reflect and review one's own practice
- To critically evaluate professional practice outcomes
- To understand basic financial and commercial principles
- To appreciate organizational cultures
- To demonstrate learning through work experience
- To adapt to new technologies
- To be aware of emotional intelligence and performance
- To express a desire to learn for oneself
- To take into account interpersonal sensitivity
- To communicate and persuade; to work with others in a team
- To assess risk and draw conclusions
- To work with information and handle a mass of diverse data
- To identify, analyze, and solve problems.

Although this list does not specifically reflect the desired thinking of graduates entering into the field of interpreting, the above list of skills equally apply to the interpreting profession. Bown (ibid.) reports that "The interpreting graduate "product" who enters the marketplace should, therefore, be able to demonstrate a range of skills and attributes that ensures that not only does the interpreter meet the national occupational and registration standards, but also is "desirable" to the community, with the potential of being "immediately employable" Fanthome (2004, p. 5)."

Given this, we suggest that assessment – and particularly summative assessment – needs to take account of these transferrable skills in addition to core competencies embedded in subject specific learning outcomes.

4.4 Assessment within interpreter training programmes

Given our discussion thus far, we can see that assessment can entail very different things. Most programmes that we are familiar with include a range of assessment types including written tests and essays, language tests, interpreting proficiency tests and reflective analyses of one's own, a peer's or a professional's work. The creation of multimedia portfolios is also gaining ground, though as with all video data, reviewing and assessment of student work is highly time consuming and thus resource intensive.

Given this, interpreter educators report interest in designing assignments that assess skills and competencies from across related domains, reflecting the fact that the tasks that student interpreters complete are complex: for example, a source language message cannot be interpreted into a sign language without considering Deaf cultural norms or the range of professional practice issues that play out in a given situation. Assessment design that evaluates skills and competencies from several domains can be beneficial for both educators and students, allowing for composite snapshots of student progress vis-à-vis the assessment criterion, namely interpreting situations in which students are confronted with authentic situations modelled on those that they will face in professional practice.

Earlier, we noted that transparency and consistency of assessment protocols is important – not just in terms of the validity of tests themselves, but also in terms of what is known as 'face validity' – that is, what the test taker believes about the test s/he must take. It is important that test-takers feel that a test is fair, relevant, robust and transparent as possible (bearing in mind that there is an argument for some minimally prepared components to be examined at given points in programmes). This is especially true for aspects of learning that are variable in nature, for example, practical placements, where, of necessity, students gain experience in a range of domains with a range of professionals, observing and participating in assignments that may vary in type, length and quality and under the supervision of professionals with varying experience. It is for this reason that the assessment of placement components demands additional attention, and potentially, additional resource commitment. Robust systems are required to ensure parity of assessment, and often this may demand that interpreter educators from the higher education institution formulate common assessment components for which grades may be moderated by input from practitioners and clients in the field.

general assessment recommendations

It is also worth pointing out that some countries work with external examiners who moderate examination processes and report back to the institution's quality assurance authority on an annual basis regarding the appropriateness and consistency of assessments that are implemented and the range of outcomes for the institution vis-a-viz other institutions offering similar educational programmes that the external examiner is familiar with. Such processes also allow for potentially very enriching dialogues to unfold between local departments and external examiners.

It goes without saying how critically important it is that interpreter educators remain abreast with best-practice developments in the field of assessment, given their privileged position at the very heart of the assessment of their courses. While not a requirement in every country at present, the goal of requiring academics to secure appropriate teaching qualifications in addition to their subject specific qualification/s is recommended as best practice and is something that our profession should work towards. Indeed, it is our hope that this document will assist in highlighting some valuable resources that may be of assistance in planning, implementing or revisiting assessment protocols.

5. Assessment

This goal of this section is to provide some discussion around a range of assessment types that are widely used in interpreter education.

5.1 Written texts assessment

Written tasks are a widely used assessment method across educational disciplines, for example; essays, exams, multiple choice testing, report and journal writing.

Within the domain of sign language interpreter training, written assessment can be used to question, test and measure knowledge and ability against defined standards in the following ways, for example:

- Demonstration of theoretical knowledge
- Articulation of opinions
- Language competency
- Critical analysis
- Reflective thinking and writing
- Text analysis and Translation tasks
- Substantial or sustained writing tasks

Tests of written knowledge are also used as a method to provide formative or summative feedback to the student on standards attained and developmental requirements. In some countries, some institutions have put in place facilities to allow Deaf students to complete what are usually delivered as written examinations in the national/regional signed language, unless the test is a evaluating competence in the written language itself (e.g. the goal is to test written English, for example).

The following are examples of evaluative assessment instruments demonstrating the written form which can be used during a sign language interpreter training programme:

- **Text analysis:** for the purposes of translation/interpretation, students can analyse written texts and incorporate justification annotations (guiding framework

assessment

examples for beginners - William P. Isham's model of Message Analysis; Roger T. Bell's 'questions' of a text (from Kipling) & Peter Newmark's text analysis/approaches to translation; or for more advanced students – Norman Fairclough's approach to Critical Discourse Analysis).

- **Exams**: for example, written scripts, multiple choice, true/false, short answer questions.

- **Journals and reflection logs**: can be used throughout a training programme to develop thinking/reflective skills and can be applied in different ways, for example, online student reflective documentation of an activity, online collaborative forum, cumulative development (formative or summative), paper-based activity.

- **Online discussion board**: new technologies provide the opportunity to evidence skills and knowledge online, via discussion forums, posting of ideas, and monitoring student participation, quality and content of responses, engagement with other students work (giving feedback).

- **Essay writing**: a proposed topic or title for students to demonstrate theoretical knowledge and their ability to analyse, organise thoughts, present evidence, synthesize ideas, critically discuss and conclude using appropriate grammar, syntax and style. Essay writing also offers students the opportunity to demonstrate their abilities in written language and topic knowledge by using a range of registers, styles and related technical terms.

- **Presentation of research findings on a given topic:** this method can be used across most domains of knowledge, individually and collectively. The presentation can incorporate mixed forms such as spoken, written text and sign language.

- **Posters:** with this method, learning outcomes from different domains of knowledge can be combined. For example, the outcomes of a research topic could be summarised and presented in a poster format.

- **Dissertations**: an evidence-based, critical discussion, for example, of an interpretation analysis or small research project.

- **Reflective portfolios on work placements:** this tool is further explained in the work placement section.

5.2 Language Tests

The efsli *Learning Outcomes for Graduates of a Three Year Interpreting Programme* establishes the following "(…) *the learning outcomes for sign language and interpreting domains of knowledge are mapped onto CEFR level C1 for receptive language skills and B2 for productive language skills. Again, we emphasise that these are the minimum threshold levels for a pass grade and this does not mean that many students may attain higher levels of proficiency(…)*"(efsli 2013*)*

The Common European Framework of Reference for Languages (CEFR) (2001) defines six levels of L2 proficiency, arranged in three bands; A1 and A2 (basic user), B1 and B2 (independent user) and C1 and C2 (proficient user). CEFR uses "can do" descriptors in a bid to move away from describing what learners cannot do, focusing instead on competence at a range of threshold levels. Critically, the CEFR is not language specific document: it can be applied to any language – and it is a point of reference which is not intended to be prescriptive.

Currently, C level descriptors are less developed than those for A and B level competencies. While proficiency is described for spoken languages in terms of listening, speaking, interacting, reading and writing, work is underway in many countries with regard to CEFR for signed languages. Work on adapting CEFR for signed languages has tended to focus on describing can-do statements at each level for learners' receptive (understanding of a signed language) and productive skills, interaction, and capacity in preparing recorded video content.

There are projects underway that are working on a European basis to adapt the CEFR descriptors for sign language teaching, learning and assessment, such as the Pro-Sign project, supported by the European Centre for Modern Languages. This project, which runs from 2012-15, aims to provide consensus driven definitions of proficiency levels for signed languages, drawing on the experience of member states who have been working with CEFR for some time in the teaching and learning of signed languages (e.g. France, Germany, Sweden, Ireland, the Netherlands, the UK, Hungary). The Pro-Signs team will provide an elaboration of curricula that focus on these levels with specifications of signed language curricula for hearing learners of a national/regional signed language for professional purposes and will develop a sample assessment kit for signed language competency at the C1/C2 level. There is also a repository available at www.cefr4sl.eu with podcasts in Interna-

assessment

tional Sign about the CEFR levels. There is also video footage (in International Sign and English) from a conference on the application of CEFR to signed languages for professional purposes (April 2013) as well as scope for sharing and discussing the experiences of interpreting programmes engaged in developing and using CEFR for teaching, learning and assessment purposes. We encourage interested readers to join the cefr4sl.eu forum, which gives free access to a range of additional resources and documents about CEFR.

With this context in mind, Professor David Little, an internationally recognised expert on CEFR and language teaching and learning, proposed some steps to be taken in order to adapt the CEFR to sign language interpreter education and training when speaking at the III efsli Working Seminar at Trinity College Dublin in February 2013. He proposes that interpreter educators:

- (1) Adapt the CEFR's taxonomic treatment of the context of use, communication themes, and communicative tasks and purposes (chapter 4) to the needs of sign language interpreters.

- (2) Adapt the relevant illustrative scales for (i) language activities (chapter 4) and (ii) the user/learner's competences (chapter 5) to sign language use.

In relation to the successive phases/modules of the education/training programme, use (1) and (2) to identify the language activities students should be able to perform at the beginning and at the end of their education, and the communicative language competences they need to develop.

Professor David Little also suggested some steps to be taken when designing a coherent system of assessment:

- Describe each assessment task that involves sign language production or interaction, drawing on relevant descriptors at the appropriate level but referring also to the course content

- Specify assessment procedures, including time allowed

- Derive assessment criteria from the relevant competence scales

- Create a rating sheet and scoring scheme

Another very useful tool is the European Language Portfolio (hereafter referred as ELP). This is a self-assessment tool developed by the Language Policy Division of the Council of Europe, but one which is also used in formative evaluation in programmes where it is used. For example, a lecturer might have a student complete an ELP sheet and then sit with them and review where the student thinks they are vis-à-vis the lecturer's evaluation of their current competency. This allows for greater appreciation on the part of educators of how a student feels they are progressing, offering a transparent, robust set of tried and tested descriptors for language competency that they can measure themselves against. It also allows for a student to identify gaps between their language competency across their working languages, offering insights into the domains and genres that they need to give further attention to in order to strengthen their linguistic repertoire.

In this way, the ELP is a document language learners can use to record and reflect on their linguistic development and their intercultural experiences. It is linked to the CEFR (users assess themselves in relation to the CEFR's proficiency levels). The ELP belongs to the learner; it is a personal document which contains three parts;

- Language passport: this summarises the owner's linguistic identity and language learning and intercultural experience. It also records the owner's self-assessment using CEFR level descriptors (A1-C2).

- Language biography: this helps the learner to set learning targets, to record and reflect on language learning and on intercultural experiences and regularly assess progress. It includes "I can" checklists to support goal setting and self-assessment.

- Dossier: this collects evidence of L2 proficiency and intercultural experience.

The ELP can be adapted to the education and training of sign language interpreters by using and adapting CEFR descriptors to sign languages and creating a version of the self-assessment grid that is appropriate to sign languages. The most challenging issue for adapting ELP to sign language is to develop C1/C2 descriptors based on real life use of sign languages, an issue that is being addressed by the Pro-Sign project; and as pointed out by Jemina Napier at the III efsli Working Seminar at Trinity College Dublin in February 2013, another challenge is that the ELP needs to account for proficiency in all working languages.

5.3 Interpreting tests

Given the focus of this document, we emphasize that this section is concerned with formative and summative interpreting tests rather than external tests run by accreditation bodies as a pathway to licensing. We note however, that in some countries undergraduate degree programmes are mapped onto national accrediting processes and as such, summative assessments may indeed serve as a pathway to national licensing for graduates of these programmes .

In Section 4 we discussed the general employability criteria that British employers report seeking in graduates, which Bown (2013) notes are equally important for interpreters. Several of the transferable skills which Bown discusses are comprised in components of interpreting tests such as critical thinking, decision making, evaluation of professional practice, and so on. Thus, what is evaluated in some tests of interpreting can go beyond knowledge of interpreting and language competency per se.

Interpreting tests may take many different forms: they may assess developing skills in paraphrasing, handling consecutively chunked components of information, extended monologues, dialogues, and they may focus on criterion from a specialist domain such as medical or legal interpreting. Interpreting tests may require a single student to complete a seen or unseen piece to camera or in a live setting or may ask that a team of students work collaboratively in a role-play which attempts to mirror authentic situations that interpreters face in the "real world".

Given such complexity – coupled with established best practice requirements for transparency, it is advisable for trainers to work with a marking rubric, that is, a rating form which lists the categories rated in a given test, along with clear rating scales that have been tried and tested and deemed reliable in advance. We include some samples in Appendix 2.

Video recordings are widely used to record sign language interpreting assessments in our field. As discussed in Section 3, face validity considerations would require that students have had the opportunity to work with any technologies that they will be assessed with in advance and that they know what criteria they are being assessed on. While we strive to ensure that interpreting tests are realistic, they can never be 'real'. As Baker (1989: 83) points out, "*any activity which takes place for the purpose of assessment is, by necessity, inauthentic.*" He goes on to add that truly authentic assessment would entail an assessor following a candidate around in a place of work for an extended period of time in a process known as *"direct assessment"*, a process that is costly and rarely feasible. Baker points out that *"All other tests differ from their real life equivalents in that the intentions of the person performing them are radically altered by the fact that he is doing a test."* This is a proviso we should bear in mind when considering the range of examination approaches commonly used in our field.

Another important consideration is how assessed content will be recorded. Any examined component on a course of study should be recorded in the interest of fairness and transparency: having a recording allows for any queries from a candidate to be discussed post-hoc with direct access to the original performance. Recording also facilitates appeals for a review of marks awarded and for established processes of second and/or external examination.

Some of the common interpreting assessment methods used across Europe include:

- **Recorded live role-plays**: many interpreting programmes work with pre-scripted role-play scenarios. While some do have fully scripted dialogues for examinations, others work with general bullet points as guidance for the key participants. This facilitates consistency of assessment for all candidates. We emphasize that best practice requires that the participants have received some training regarding what the goal of the role-play is and that they have the opportunity to run through the role play scenario several times before the assessment commences so that they are comfortable in their roles. In formative assessment processes, lecturers can provide feedback on student performances, students can review and evaluate their own work and/or work on peer-evaluations with respect to the rubrics that will be applied to their performances in summative assessments. Role plays allow assessment of the dialogic, interactive triangle dynamic, to evaluate management of turn-taking, communication repair, and to assess a number of elements of a communication; and can also be used for assessment of multi-party discourse (e.g., meetings) at more advanced stages.

- **Pre-recorded monologues and dialogues:** in this kind of assessment, a student works from a prepared monologue or dialogue as the source text. In the case of Deaf student interpreters, this approach can include working from subtitled content into a local/regional signed language or into International Sign. Such materials also facilitate access for Deaf interpreter educators contributing to a programme. Pre-recorded resources also provide consistent source language materials for a larger cohort of students and is less resource intensive than live role plays. The downside is that assessors cannot evaluate how a student is interacting with and responding to live participants as they could in a live role play.

- **Placement learning inside the university/college**: Some institutions attempt to establish a form of direct assessment whereby a student is assessed while they interpret for each other and other lecturers. This can be carefully crafted to function as a pseudo-authentic assessment – that is, it can be somewhere between role-play and real life but in a safe environment with the benefit of feedback. Working within one's own institution may help in negotiating issues around securing permission from all participants for a student interpreter to undertake interpreting, to be observed/recorded, and to be assessed on their performance in this situation.

- **Monologue and dialogue recordings;** students' output is recorded to allow teachers and students to 'playback' the recording and see things that might be missed when observing live. It allows the assessment of instantaneous spontaneous communications.

- **Direct feedback from consumers in live interpreting situations**; in the case of Deafblind consumers, this might be especially important. Clearly, there are obstacles to consider (practical, resource-wise and ethically) around seeking to assess students in truly authentic settings as permissions would have to be secured in advance from all parties to the event and the recording of an event would impinge on the confidentiality of the participants as a matter of course. These issues have to be weighed up in planning for live assessments along with considerations around consistency of assessment protocols (are all students being assessed on the same things if all assessment settings are different?) and rater reliability (are all assessors trained in how to rate and provide feedback for such examinations? Can you guarantee inter- and intra-rater reliability?) Some programmes have built in protocols for participants in authentic settings to feed into the assessment process, but trained raters are responsible for coordinating grading.

- **Think aloud protocols (TAP):** Some programmes include reflexive analysis of performance as part of their assessment protocol. In such instances, a student records themselves while they review their interpreting performance. The student can be instructed to stop the video recording of their performance whenever they wish to comment on what they were thinking or trying to accomplish with a target language output, for example. They can be invited to comment on whether they feel they were successful in their decision making or if there were alternatives that they feel would have worked better. They might wish to focus on how they managed their processing time ('lag time') or how they managed their attention across the piece (using, for example, Daniel Gile's Effort Model (1995)).

- **Write-it-down protocol using ELAN:** An alternative to the TAP that has been used is a process whereby students review their performance in ELAN, the freely available software programme developed by the Max Planx Institute, Nijmegan now widely used in sign linguistics research, and increasingly in interpreter education programmes. Students can be advised to time-align their commentary to their performance by tagging segments of the interpretation that they deem to be of note. Working with ELAN facilitates the opportunity for lecturers to feedback in kind, creating a document that can facilitate a dialogue between student and lecturer. For discussion on how ELAN can be used in interpreter education, see Leeson (2008) and Goswell, (2012).

5.4 Interpreting Portfolio

"An e-portfolio is the product, created by the learner, a collection of digital artefacts articulating experiences, achievements and learning"

JISC 2008:6

A portfolio is a collection of student work created for the purposes of demonstrating progressive learning or showcasing their best work, and can be used to assess various domains of knowledge. It is a useful tool for the reflection and evidence of skills development, and can provide a method to examine and measure progress by documenting the process of learning or change as it occurs. Portfolios can extend beyond test scores to include substantive examples of student engagement, experience and achievement. For example, Grosvenor (1993) describes three models of portfolio:

- The showcase model: work samples chosen by student;
- The descriptive model: representative work of student, with no attempt at evaluation;
- The evaluative model: representative products that have been evaluated by criteria.

assessment

Each of these three models could be used throughout an interpreter education programme at any time for formative and summative assessment purposes, although the ideal would be to combine the showcase and the evaluative models to encourage critical and reflective practice. We can also note that some programmes ask students to present all work completed as a component of a combined showcase/evaluative portfolio as a mechanism for tracking student participation, reflection and development over time.

Portfolios have the capacity to be flexible, personal, learner-centred, portable (e-portfolio) accessible to the student/external bodies and created at key times of the learner's journey. They can promote lifelong learning aspirations, personal development planning (current and future), the setting/achievement of defined goals, can incorporate tutor feedback one to one, or contributions where several parties are involved e.g. placement, community volunteering experiences, supervisory reports. For prospective employers, they can be a useful evidence tool of the individual's skills, abilities and accomplishments.

As with other forms of assessment, portfolios need to be structured according to demonstration of learning competencies, with clear assessment frameworks (i.e. criteria) for students to collect evidence for, otherwise the portfolio can become unwieldy.

Portfolios can be presented as a paper-based collection of written examples but increasingly portfolios are developed electronically during training programmes: *"An e-portfolio, like its paper equivalent, is produced at key points in a learning journey – for example, when demonstrating the outcomes of learning, applying for a job or the next stage of learning or seeking registration with a professional body. e-Portfolios demonstrate what is important about individuals at particular points in time – their achievements, reflections on learning and, potentially, a rich and rounded picture of their abilities, aspirations and ambitions."* (JISC 2008:6)

With a defined purpose, they can be embedded throughout the programme in different modules or units of study and reflect the evidence of successfully working towards or achieving the learning outcomes.

assessment

The following are examples of materials that can be included within the portfolio:

- **Reflective thinking and writing - written/signed/narrative/audio.** This can be described as a 'Diary or Learning Journal' and can be compiled on a regular basis e.g. weekly, post an 'event/learning experience'.

- **Academic essays**

- **Analyses (critiques) of case studies/ literature** e.g. researching content and compiling a summary or annotation

- **Preparation materials/ discourse maps/mind maps**

- **Self evaluation of performance on a particular task**

- **Diagnostic analysis** e.g. interpreting and sign language performance

- **Peer evaluation e.g. class performance of a task, feedback given for online homework, team working**

- **Problem based Learning (PBL)** (e.g. class based role-plays, hypothesis of a situation/dilemma, critical and creative thinking)

- **Group work** (e.g. where the objective is leadership of a task and evidence of collaboration and performance through peer feedback)

- **Lecturer feedback** (written/spoken/signed)

- **Mark grids** (grades achieved, formative/summative feedback)

- **Transcripts of a sign language into a written language** (written translation)

- **Written text into a sign language** (sight translation)

- **General translation exercises,** e.g. discussions around finding equivalence and justifications

- **Observation and evaluation of other interpreters**; this can be a constructive critique e.g. class/peer work against a taught framework of enquiry, placement learning experiences (content must be anonymous and with permission of those involved)

- **Video evidence of a performance:** speech to sign language and sign language to speech

- **Video evidence using ELAN:** a professional computer programme that allows annotations to be mapped against video clips of sign language. A useful diagnostic and feedback tool for students and tutors.

assessment

- **Digital media:** Speaker interpreted presentations, podcasts, sign language and interpreting examples (speech/sign), spoken critiques, images, etc.
- **Annotated bibliographies**
- **Inclusion of interpreting think-aloud protocols** (as discussed in section 4.3)
- **Hyperlinking of resources to enhance portfolio**
- **Student 'blogs'** to show progressive thinking/learning and/or shared learning
- **Personal or retrospective statement** (e.g. at different levels of development)
- **Creation of e.g. Poster from a research topic, informative leaflet/booklet/guide**

Depending on the design of this assessment, evaluation of portfolios may require that students participate in an interview with one of their teachers to discuss their portfolio content. An example of an end-of-programme portfolio structure could look something like this:

- Personal profile
    - ⇒ Language Passport
    - ⇒ Language biography
- Dossier:
    - ⇒ Evidence of interpreter assignment preparation
    - ⇒ Evidence of interpreting skills (monologic & dialogic)
    - ⇒ Evidence of interpreter evaluations (self, peer, teacher, mentor)
    - ⇒ Evidence of critical learning (e.g., reflective journals, blogs)
    - ⇒ Evidence of application of theory to practice (e.g., essays)

assessment

5.5 Placement Learning

Placement learning is an essential part of the overall programme of study by providing the opportunity to contextualise theoretical knowledge, abstract discussion and simulated learning, by the practical application of observational and interpreting skills. It takes place within a learning environment which is external to the training provider, e.g. interpreting service within a Deaf organisation, privately owned/managed interpreting agency, educational settings, freelance interpreter, and the module or unit of study will have clearly defined and assessed learning outcomes which relate to the overall design of the interpreter education programme. These learning outcomes must be flexible enough to appropriately accommodate the diversity of placement settings which a cohort of students may encounter during a formalised placement learning experience.

The overall programme design will clearly state where placement learning is to take place e.g. during each year of study, or at certain periods throughout the programme such as during the final year before graduation. A clear distinction must be made between activities that form part of the training programme and those which are encouraged as external to it, for example; some interpreter education programmes encourage students to participate in volunteering experiences within an organisation such as administration duties, social activities, workshop participation in the role of 'assistant' under the auspices of the organisation's supervisory frameworks. These can be seen as a reciprocal developmental activity or 'service learning' experience, as opposed to formalised placement learning with agreed goals and assessed outcomes. Both types of learning experiences can form part of a student's stepped development but require clearly communicated design frameworks as to which are being assessed and which are not (Bown 2013).

Within a given training programme, placement components can take many different forms and their design and position within the programme will be influenced by a range of internal (educational institution/programme design parameters, available resources) and external factors such as economic resources and social support structures.

Placement learning can be delivered in various ways, for example, as, co-op education, apprenticeships, internships, externships, Erasmus work placements, job shadowing opportunities, virtual internships and work-based learning. Definitions of each of these terms can be found in the Glossary at the end of this document.

assessment

Two other definitions of placement, focusing on a community versus industry base that may be useful are community placement and work placement:

Community placement concentrates more on 'immersion' experiences that are typically required of spoken language interpreting students who go and live in a country that uses the target language, which they are learning as their L2. The goal of a community placement is for students to use their L2 on an everyday basis in a range of contexts, and to work in a non-interpreting role, for example as a support worker in a deaf school, or administration assistant in a deaf service-provider organisation. This placement experience would enable students to develop greater fluency in the sign language skills, and their knowledge and understanding of intercultural communication issues between deaf and hearing people. The work placement would focus on giving students an opportunity to develop their interpreting skills either by being based in an interpreting agency or shadowing a freelance interpreter, and having the chance to try interpreting in safe environments and under supervision.

Others adopt a 'service learning' approach to embedding engagement with the Deaf community as a core part of the interpreter education programme (Shaw, 2013), which can either be part of formalised placement learning experience (i.e., *community placement*) or within structured credit-based subjects, or both; with agreed goals and assessed outcomes. Service learning and placement learning introduces students to experiential as well as classroom learning, whereby they are expected to participate in community and interpreting activities and are encouraged to be engaged and ethical citizens. Within service learning in particular, students learn about "the significance of membership in a community while reflecting on the importance of reciprocity and the symbiotic nature of learning and living" (Monikowski & Peterson, 1995, p.195).

Staffing and supervision during the placement learning experience

Placement structure and resources (e.g. number of staff involved, level of qualification and experience, finance available to placement sites and students) will influence the design and application of the placement experience. Ideally, both Higher Education Institution (HEI) educators and placement site supervisors will hold the same level of qualification (interpreting, teacher training, mentoring/coaching)

assessment

and field experience. However, the reality is that this may not always be the case. Where this occurs, then the HEI has responsibility to ensure that placement site supervisors receive induction and training as to the requirements, responsibilities and standards expected of them. They should also be kept in close contact with the HEI during the placement period.

Where such diversity of learning experience exists, then ultimately it is the HEI that should hold responsibility for the actual graded assessment process (theory and practice). Dependent upon the design of the programme, this can for example in the context of live interpreting skills, take place at the placement site and be carried out by or in conjunction with, HEI staff or within the HEI itself as a simulated role-play activity that mirrors a site experience. It is important to remember that the students should have parity of experience within the assessment process, i.e. , clearly defined outcomes, quality of task, consistency of content, duration, exam conditions and feedback (Bown 2012, 2013)

Administration of placement learning, student support frameworks & supervision

Well designed and organised placement learning requires sufficient resources that adequately reflect the processes involved, (i.e. educators, administration staff and appropriate allocation of time) for it to be an effective and meaningful experience for students, the Deaf community and placement sites. It should ideally be managed and administered by the HEI, which in turn provides one reference point for communication, documentation, induction, maintenance, evaluation and the processes of insurance, health and safety, risk assessment and quality control.

Resources, placement opportunities, site supervisor availability and the levels of qualification and experience may vary across interpreter training programmes and placement sites. However, a flexible yet robust approach is required to ensure quality and parity of the student experience in line with the HEI programme requirements. A way to construct one aspect of support (e.g. the articulation of reflective thinking and writing) is by the 'triangulation' of supervisory arrangements between placement supervisors, students and the HEI interpreter educators. For example, the allocated placement site supervisors can facilitate the reflective discussions on observed or worked interpreting assignments and view/discuss any reflective written work the student produces for the module or unit of study on a daily/weekly basis. The team of HEI educators should then undertake supervision (on a rotational basis) of discussed and documented learning experiences (e.g. for the outcome of a 'Diary' or 'Learning Journal') for the duration of the placement process at the HEI. The student should, at least every 2-3 weeks, meet with their institutional HEI educational supervisor for a minimum of 30 minutes for a dedicated one to one period which gives the opportunity to discuss the learning experiences, review and provide written and verbal feedback on submitted reflective written work and check progress against the overall module/unit learning and assessment outcome requirements (Bown 2012, 2013).

Assessment

A broad variety of mechanisms can be used to evaluate a student's achievements during her/his placement period. We refer readers to the QAA (2012) for discussion of key precepts of relevance to the preparation of assessment in this domain.

Some examples of assessment instruments for placement and service learning are listed below:

- **Reflective learning 'journals'/'diaries'**: these can follow a given 'template' to promote the contextualisation, thinking and reflection upon the observed or worked interpreting assignment. In the early stages of reflective writing, a framework helps guide student development, provides parity amongst a cohort, and allows a more standardised approach to feedback from all tutors involved. Within the design of the module/unit, tutors can decide whether to ask students to contrast their reflective thinking with current sources of literature to justify the options, decisions and conclusions they cite from their experiences (Bown 2013).

- **Portfolio collection of activities/evidence**; for example they can appendix research they have carried out prior to observing/working an interpreting assignment, written feedback from deaf/hearing clients, supervisory feedback, related experiences such as learning about the administration tasks relevant to their domain, (e.g. booking of interpreters, processing paperwork/online) if they are situated in an interpreting agency.

- **Recorded evidence of interpreting skills**; can be simulated or non-simulated. Where a student is to record their own performance in an authentic situation, they must be obliged to seek consent from all stakeholders. Clearly there is a challenge in the collection of authentic data whereby institutions training interpreters must negotiate between authenticity in placement learning assessment and the intrusion on stakeholders. Data protection legislation and the confidentiality of clients must be respected at every step in any such process.

- **Feedback from site supervisors on a range of areas**: interpersonal skills, interpreting skills, time keeping/punctuality, relationship to clients, impact/consequences of decisions/actions, can be used as a guide to student performance and behaviour on a placement. It should not however, due to the diversity of qualification/experience of placement supervisor, be a graded assessment piece.

- **Feedback used as a development tool**: feedback from a range of sources (e.g. spoken, written, signed) can be reflected upon with the site supervisor and HEI educator. Personal development goals can be reviewed and adjusted in line with feedback received.

- **Use of feedback from all consumers as evidence**: can be incorporated into a portfolio of learning.

- **Site visits by HEI educators**: these can have more than one purpose, e.g. to check on student progress, watch a student interpreted assignment, assess a performance for specific purposes, provide evidence for live formative or summative feedback

- **Potential to show exposure to 'specific settings'**: (placement opportunities permitting) e.g. interpreting for exams or tests (e.g. driving test), team interpreting, legal, mental health settings.

- **Use of Interviews (sometimes called "Vivas" or "Oral Exams"), Exams, Question and Answer sessions, presentations**: for example, students can be asked to present briefly on a key topic such as 'fitness to practice' or 'professional standards' and link this to their work experience. A panel of examiners can then ask questions about the student's learning while on placement, their short-term goals and their medium to long term continuing educational practice plans. There is also scope to have students present in their L2 as a mechanism for also examining language capacity at a higher level (see also Section 5.2)

- **Community projects**: whereby students work on service learning projects in collaboration with deaf individuals or deaf organisations that directly benefit the community (e.g., translation of information materials, organisation of community event, individual/collaborative small scale research tasks).

6. Glossary

Apprenticeship:

Work-based training, usually full-time and paid (if not very highly). Apprentices often work towards a vocational qualification, and are generally in more hands-on roles.

Basic skills:

Also referred to as 'generic', 'key' or 'core' skills, basic skills are not specific to a particular job, but needed by most employers. The main ones are: literacy, numeracy, basic IT skills, and good communication.

Co-operative education ('co-op'):

Work placements provided through partnerships between a higher education institution and businesses or other organizations. These are usually assessed, allowing students to gain course credits.

CV (curriculum vitae):

Referred to as a résumé in some regions, a CV is summary of your work experience, education and other skills and qualifications to date; used to give potential employers a quick overview and highlight personal and professional strengths.

Employer Guide:

A document produced by the School/Division to provide guidance to support employers during the work-based periods of a student's programme.

Erasmus work placement:

A work placement completed with funding from the European Union's **Erasmus scheme**, which promotes student mobility within Europe. Placements must last between three and twelve months, be relevant to the student's course, and be in a participating European country. The term Erasmus is an abbreviation of the European Community Action Scheme for the Mobility of University Students.

glossary

Experiential learning:

Learning through experience. This could include work placements, but also practical projects completed within a HEI.

Externship:

Sometimes used interchangeably with 'internship', but usually refers specifically to a work experience opportunity arranged by a HEI, rather than individual students. This could be a work placement, visit from a professional, job shadowing or a research project in collaboration with a business.

HEI:

Higher Education Institution

Hard skills:

In contrast to 'soft skills' (see below), 'hard skills' are not about interactions with people, but refer to an individual's ability to complete technical and mental tasks – for example, being able to handle complex data, knowing how to use relevant software, or operating a machine.

Internship:

Often used interchangeably with 'work experience' (see below), but usually referring to 'white-collar' jobs. Internships are often paid, and may last significantly longer than work experience placements.

Job shadowing:

A type of work experience which involves observing a professional going about their normal work routine, to get an idea of what the role is like.

Mentor:

An experienced professional who is assigned to a 'mentee' (less experienced) to advise him or her on how to achieve career goals.

glossary

Placement:

Any activity or experience that involves the student in placement-related learning. This might include actual work experience, simulation, talking to clients, attending seminars, undertaking research, etc. The student may or may not have a say in choosing the placement.

Placement Learning (PL):

Placement Learning is regarded as the learning achieved during an agreed and negotiated period of learning that takes place outside the institution at which the full or part-time student is enrolled or engaged in learning.

Placement Learning Handbook:

Document / website/ or equivalent containing Placement Learning information. (May be combined with information for Work-based Learning).

Placement Provider:

The organisation or individual accepting a student for a period of Placement Learning. This may be as a paid employee or as a student on work experience. It may be on a day release basis, as a year out, or in blocks of experience.

Risk Assessment:

The process of identifying hazards and the risks associated with them.

Service-learning:

Similar to cooperative learning (see above), but based on **serving the local community** in some way, by working with non-profit, philanthropic, community and public sector organizations.

Soft skills:

Definitions vary, but generally 'soft skills' are interpersonal – how good you are at getting on with people, communicating, making a good impression and the like. These are often at least equally as important as hard skills (see above).

glossary

Specific skills:

Skills needed for a particular job or sector of employment. For example, specific language competencies and or qualifications for working as an interpreter in a given region. Employers usually include a list of the most important specific skills when advertising vacancies.

Supervisor:

Individual from the work-based / placement provider organisation who provides support and guidance to the student and, where appropriate, assessment of the student whilst on placement /in work-based learning.

Tutor:

Individual member of academic staff who is employed by the HEI (or partner institute) to support and advise the student on academic and related matters.

Virtual internship:

An internship you can do from anywhere, by using internet, email, phone and other media to communicate and submit work.

Work-based Learning (WBL):

Is a learning process which focuses university level critical thinking upon work (paid or unpaid) in order to facilitate the recognition, acquisition and application of individual and collective knowledge, skills and abilities, to achieve specific outcomes of significance to the learner, their work and the university. (Garnett, 2004)

Work-based Learning Handbook:

Document / website/ or equivalent containing Schools' / Divisions' Placement Learning information. (May be combined with information for Placement Learning).

glossary

Work experience:

Often used interchangeably with 'internship' (see above). A period of work at a business in order to gain experience of that industry. May be paid or unpaid.

7. References

- Angelelli, Claudia, and Holly Jackobson 2009: Introduction, Testing and Assessment in Translation and Interpreting Studies. A Call for Dialogue Betweeen Research and Practice. Testing and Assessment in Translation and Interpreting Studies. A Call for Dialogue Betweeen Research and Practice. edited by C. Angelelli and Holly Jackobson Amsterdam and Philadelphia: John Benjamins.

- Baker, David 1989: Language Testing: A Critical Survey and Practical Guide. London: Edward Arnold.

- Bell. R.T. 1991: Translation and Translating: Theory and Practice, New York: Longman.

- Bown, Sarah 2013: "Autopoiesis: Scaffolding the Reflective Practitioner toward Employability." International Journal of Interpreter Education (IJIE) 5, no. 1 (2013): 51-63.

- Bown, Sarah 2013: Assessing Placement Learning: Closing the gap between theoretical constructs and professional practice. Round table presentation at: III efsli Working Seminar, Trinity College, Dublin, 27 & 28 February 2013.

- Bown, Sarah 2012: Reality Bites! Making it real within the context of an interpreter training programme: Paper presented at: efsli Trainers'Seminar, ITAT, University of Graz, 17th-19th September 2012.

- Bown, Sarah, and K. Dekesel 2011: "The Citoyen Interpreter. " In Paper presented at the 3rd Community Interpreting Research Seminar. Trinity College Dublin, Ireland.

- Bown, Sarah and K. Dekesel 2009: "Reflection in Practice: Developing and Embedding Students' Reflection for Professional Practice and Employability - the Student Perspective". In Paper presented at the 3rd Employability Conference. Wolverhampton, UK.

- Bown, Sarah and K. Dekesel 2010: "The Reflective Interpreter as Global Citizen." Paper presented at: efsli annual conference. Glasgow, UK,11th & 12th September 2010 .

- Council of Europe 2001: Common European Framework of Reference for Languages: Learning, Teaching, Assessment. Cambridge: Cambridge University Press.

- De Wit, Maya. 2012: Sign Language Interpreting in Europe, 2012 edition. Self-published. Printed by Create Space. Baarn: M. de Wit

- efsli, 2013: Learning Outcomes for Graduates of a Three Year Interpreting Programme. Self-published. Brussels: European Forum of Sign Language Interpret-

references

ers.

- Fairclough, N. 1992: Discourse and social change. Oxford: Polity Press.

- Gile, Daniel 1995:. Basic Concepts and Models for Interpreter and Translator Training. Amsterdam: John Benjamins.

- Goswell, D. 2012: Do you see what I see? Using ELAN for self-analysis and reflection. International Journal of Interpreter Education, 4(1), 73-82.

- Grosvenor, L.1993: Taking assessment matters into our own hands. In M. Dalheim (Ed.), Student portfolios (NEA Professional Library Teacher-to-Teacher Series). Washington DC: Bookshelf (Editorial Projects in Education).

- Isham. W. P. 1986: The Role of Message Analysis in Interpretation in McIntire, M. L. (ed.) Interpreting: The Art of Cross Cultural Mediation, USA, Silver Spring: RID publications pp. 111-122.

- JISC. 2008: "Effective Practice with E-Portfolios, Supporting 21st Century Learning ". http://www.jisc.ac.uk/media/documents/publications/effectivepracticeeportfolios.pdf: JISC.

- Johnston, Trevor, and Onno Crasborn 2006: "The Use of Elan Annotation Software in the Creation of Signed Language Corpora, ." In Proceedings of the EMELD'06 Workshop on Digital Language Documentation: Tools and Standards: The State of the Art. Lansing: MI: http://emeld.org/workshop/2006/papers/johnston-crasborn.pdf.

- Little, David 2013: The Common European Framework of Reference for Languages and its relevance to sign language interpreter training programmes. Keynote speech at: III efsli Working Seminar, Trinity College, Dublin, 27 & 28 February 2013.

- Leeson, Lorraine 2011:"Mark My Words: The Linguistic, Social and Political Significance of the Assessment of Signed Language Interpreters." In *Advances in Interpreting Research: Inquiry in Action*, edited by Brenda Nicodemus and Laurie Swabey, 153-76. Amsterdam and Philadelphia: John Benjamins.

- Leeson, Lorraine 2008: "Quantum Leap - Leveraging the Signs of Ireland Digital Corpus in Irish Sign Language/English Interpreter Training." *The Sign Language Translator and Interpreter* 2, no. 2 (2008): 149-76.

- Leeson, Lorraine, and Deirdre Byrne-Dunne 2009: "Applying the Common European Reference Framework to the Teaching, Learning and Assessment of Signed Languages." In D-Signs: Distance online training in sign language (UK/08/LLP-LdV/TOI/163_141). Dublin: Trinity College Dublin.

references

- Leeson, Lorraine, and Carmel Grehan 2010: "A Common European Framework for Sign Language Curricula? D-Sign(Ing) a Curriculum Aligned to the Common European Framework of Reference." In Sign Language Teaching and Learning, edited by Maria Mertzani, 21-33. Bristol: Centre for Deaf Studies University of Bristol.

- McNamara, T. F. 2000: Language Testing. Oxford: Oxford University Press, 2000.

- Monikowski, Christine, & Rico Peterson 2005: Service learning in interpreting education: A sense of place. In M. Marschark, R. Peterson & E. A. Winston (Eds.), *Interpreting and interpreting education: Directions for research and practice* (pp. 188-207). New York, USA: Oxford University Press.

- Newmark, P. 1988: A Textbook of Translation, Hemel Hemstead: Prentice Hall.

- Niska, Helge 1999: "Testing Community Interpreters: A Theory, a Model and a Plea for Research." In Liaison Interpreting in the Community, edited by Mabel Erasmus, 278-87. Pretoria: Van Schaik.

- Nonhebel, Annika, Onno Crasborn, and Els van der Kooij 2004: "Sign Language Transcription Conventions for the Echo Project." http://www.let.kun.nl/sign-lang/echo/docs/transcr_conv.pdf.

- Pochhacker, F. 2004: Introducing Interpreting Studies. London and New York: Routeledge.

- QAA, Q. A. A. f. H. E. 2007: Code of practice for the assurance of academic quality and standards in higher education. Section 9: Work-based and placement learning. York, QAA.

- Salaets, Heidi, and Myriam Vermeerbergen 2011: "Assessing Students on Completion of Community Interpreting Training: How to Reshape Theoretical Concepts for Practice?". In Modelling the Field of Community Interpreting: Questions of Methodology in Research and Training, edited by Claudia Kainz, Erich Prunc and Rafael Schogler. Representation - Transformation, 152-77. Vienna: Lit Verlag.

- Sawyer, David. B. 2004, Fundamental Aspects of Interpreter Education. Curriculum and Assessment. Amsterdam and Philadelphia: John Benjamins.

- Shaw, Sherry 2013: Service learning in interpreter education: Strategies for extending student involvement in the Deaf community. Washington, DC: Gallaudet University Press.

- The Quality Assurance Agency for Higher Education (QAA) 2012: Understand-

references

ing Assessment: Its Role in Safeguarding Academic Standards and Quality in Higher Education. A Guide for Early Career Staff. Gloucester: The Quality Assurance Agency for Higher Education.

- University of Wolverhampton 2008: Work-based and Placement Learning Guidelines. Wolverhampton: UQC.

Websites

- CEFR for Signed Languages: http://www.cefr4sl.eu [Information available in English and in International Sign] (accessed 10 October 2013)

- Common European Framework of Reference for Languages (CEFR): www.coe.int/t/dg4/education/elp/elp-reg/cefr_EN.asp (accessed 15 September 2013)

- ELAN [is a free resource which can be downloaded at]: http://tla.mpi.nl/tools/tla-tools/elan/ (accessed 20 October 2013)

- European Language Portfolio: www.coe.int/t/dg4/education/elp/ (accessed 15 September 2013)

- Garnett, J. 2004. Inaugural lecture. http://www.mdx.ac.uk/wbl/cfe/faqs.asp. (accessed 13November 2013)

- Pro-Signs Project: www.ecml.at/F5/Abstract/tabid/868/language/en-GB/Default.aspx [Information available in English and in International Sign] (accessed 15 October 2013)

- Top Universities http://www.topuniversities.com/student-info/careers-advice/getting-job-after-university-glossary (accessed 15 October 2013)

Appendix 1: Further resources

European Level:

European Higher Education Area (EHEA):

EHEA was launched along with the Bologna Process' decade anniversary, in March 2010. As the main objective of the Bologna Process since its inception in 1999, the EHEA was meant to ensure more comparable, compatible and coherent systems of higher education in Europe. Between 1999 - 2010, all the efforts of the Bologna Process members were targeted to creating the European Higher Education Area, that became reality with the Budapest-Vienna Declaration of March, 2010. The next decade will be aimed at consolidating the EHEA and thus the current EHEA permanent website will play a key role in this process of intense internal and external communication. For more information about the Bologna Process see: www.ehea.info

European Association for Quality Assurance in Higher Education (ENQA):

ENQA disseminates information, experiences and good practices in the field of quality assurance (QA) in higher education to European QA agencies, public authorities and higher education institutions. For more on this issue see: www.enqa.eu. A list of national, regional and international quality assurance in higher education affiliates of ENQA can be found at: www.enqa.eu/affil.lasso

Tuning Educational Structures in Europe:

TUNING Educational Structures in Europe started in 2000 as a project to link the political objectives of the Bologna Process and at a later stage the Lisbon Strategy to the higher educational sector. Over time Tuning has developed into a Process, an approach to (re-)designing, develop, implement, evaluate and enhance quality first, second and third cycle degree programmes. The Tuning outcomes as well as its tools are presented in a range of Tuning publications, which institutions and their academics are invited to test and use in their own setting. The Tuning approach has been developed by and is meant for higher education institutions: www.unideusto.org/tuningeu/

Qrossroads

Qrossroads presents information regarding quality assured and accredited

appendix 1

higher education in Europe. The information on Qrossroads is provided by quality assurance and accreditation agencies and specifically concerns qualifications from quality assured and accredited programmes and institutions. See: www.qrossroads.eu/quality-assurance-and-accreditation

Supplementary National Resources of Interest:

In English:

- **ASET (Work-Based and Placement Learning Association)** The body that represents the placement and employability practitioners. www.asetonline.org/
- Brown, Sally. Assessment for Learning. Learning and Teaching in Higher Education, Issue 1, 2004-05. 81-89.
- **CILT** – The national centre for languages: cilt.org.uk/home.aspx
- **The Higher Education Academy:** www.heacademy.ac.uk
- The Higher Education Academy 2012: A Marked Improvement: Transforming Assessment in Higher Education. www.heacademy.ac.uk/resources/detail/assessment/a-marked-improvement
- The Higher Education Academy Subject Benchmark Statements [link brings you to statements for "Languages and Related Studies"]: http://www.qaa.ac.uk/Publications/InformationAndGuidance/Pages/Subject-benchmark-statement-Languages-and-related-studies.aspx
- **QAA - Quality Assurance Agency for Higher Education** The Agency's mission is to promote public confidence that quality of provision and standards of awards in higher education are being safeguarded and enhanced. www.qaa.ac.uk/Pages/default.aspx
- **SEDA - Staff and Educational Development Association** SEDA is the professional association for staff and educational developers in the UK, promoting innovation and good practice in higher education. www.seda.ac.uk/
- **SQA - Scottish Qualifications Authority**. Guide to Assessment (2009). http://www.sqa.org.uk/files_ccc/GuideToAssessment.pdf
- **UKCOSA: The Council for International Education** is an independent, not-for-profit organisation committed to promoting educational mobility and

providing support to international students and the professionals who work with them.

- www.intstudy.com/study-in-uk/study-advice/ukcosa-the-council-for-international-education

In German:

- **Landesschulamt und Lehrkräfteakademie** http://lehrerbildung.lsa.hessen.de/irj/AfL_Internet?uid=76440311-ad5b-d411-1010-43bf5aa60dfa

In Polish (with some content in English):

- **Stowarzyszenie Tłumaczy Polskiego Języka Migowego**

    www.stpjm.org.pl

In Turkish and English:

- www.tyyc.yok.gov.tr/

Resources Related to Placement Learning

- A Good Practice Guide for Placement and Other Work-Based Learning Opportunities in Higher Education. 2009. www.asetonline.org/documents/ASETCodeofPractice-Version2.1_000.pdf
- Pegg, A., Waldock, J., Hendy-Isaac, S., & Lawton, R. 2012: Pedagogy for employability. York, UK: The Higher Education Academy. http://www.heacademy.ac.uk/assets/documents/employability/pedagogy_for_employability_update_2012.pdf

appendix 1

- QAA - The Quality Assurance Agency Code of Practice for the assurance of academic quality and standards in higher education. Section 9: Work-based and placement learning, September 2007.

- http://www.qaa.ac.uk/Publications/InformationAndGuidance/Pages/Code-of-practice-Section-9.aspx [See also the Quality Code at: http://www.qaa.ac.uk/AssuringStandardsAndQuality/quality-code/Pages/Quality-Code-Part-B.aspx]

- The National Council for Work Experience - Student Guide http://www.asetonline.org/documents/NCWEStudentGuide.pdf

- Universities UK - Preparing Graduates for the World of Work http://www.asetonline.org/documents/CBIandUUK-FutureFit-PreparingGraduatesfortheWorldofWork.pdf

Appendix 2: Sample matrices and semi scripted role play

In this appendix you can find the following documents:

- ***Postgraduate Diploma in Auslan / English Interpreting at Macquarie University, Sydney, Australia***

    ⇒ Auslan-English monologic TT assessment

- ***Bachelor in Deaf Studies (ISL/English Interpreting) (hons.) at the Centre for Deaf Studies, Trinity College Dublin, Ireland***

    ⇒ Simultaneous Interpreting 1 ISL/English Marking Rubric

    ⇒ Simultaneous Interpreting 1 English/ISL Marking Rubric

    ⇒ Simultaneous Interpreting 2 Marking Rubric

    ⇒ Liaison Interpreting Exam – sample scripted role-play with notes for hearing and deaf participants and student.

- ***B.A. (hons.) Interpreting BSL/English Programme at the University of Wolverhampton, UK***

    ⇒ L6 BSL to English Interpreting Master Matrix

    ⇒ L6 English to BSL Interpreting Master Matrix

    ⇒ L6 BSL Language Master Matrix

    ⇒ L5 Text Analysis Master Matrix

    ⇒ L3 Basic BSL Matrix

Macquarie University Postgraduate Diploma in Auslan/ English Interpreting

Auslan-English monologic TT assessment

STUDENT: _____

TT PRODUCTION (English) /15%

Comfortable speed/ pace
Appropriate voice projection & volume
Confident demeanour
No distracting mannerisms
Clear pronunciation

TT STRUCTURE & FLUENCY (English) /30%

Sufficient lexical range
Natural target language syntax & grammar
Appropriate prosody (intonation, pauses, etc)
Cohesive and coherent ideas
Comfortable to listen to (flow)

MESSAGE PROCESSING A-E /25%

Comprehension of ST message/ concepts
Comprehension of ST fingerspelling & numbers
Effective use of timelag
Strategic use of omissions, additions, substitutions
Appropriate free/literal decisions
Efficient recovery from errors

ACCURATE TRANSFER A-E /30%

Equivalent ST content/ concepts represented in TT
Equivalent affect
Appropriate register
Cultural adjustment/s

General comments:

Score: Grade: Assessor/s _____   Date: _____

© D.Goswell, M.Leneham & J.Napier, 2010

Centre for Deaf Studies, Trinity College Dublin

Simultaneous Interpreting 1 Exam 2012-13 ENG > ISL

STUDENT NAME: _____ Student No. _____

Assessed by (please tick): Prof. Lorraine Leeson ☐ Ms. Teresa Lynch ☐ Ms. Sarah Sheridan ☐

Signed _____ Dated _____

Marking Descriptors

1	**F= Seriously Inadequate** performance does not in any way meet the minimum requirements for performance. There are **serious problems** with TL production (e.g. grammatical structure is inappropriate or lacking with many instances of source language intrusion), translation issues (e.g. lack of accuracy in message transfer, very poor awareness of function, register, etc.). Overall product is unsatisfactory.
2	**III= Borderline** performance, but, with further input, may reach target required. There are **problems with some target domains** such as TL production (e.g. grammatical structure is inappropriate with many instances of source language intrusion), translation issues (e.g. lack of accuracy in message transfer, very poor awareness of function, register, etc.). Overall product is borderline pass.
3	**II.2 = Adequate performance** in terms of target language production, translation issues, etc. This performance meets the minimum standard required though work is needed to improve skill level across several of the target domains.
4	**II.1 = Good performance** in terms of target language production and translating issues. There are instances across the target domains where further skill development is required.
5	**I = Excellent performance** in terms of target language production and translating issues. There are rare instances across the target domains where further skill development is required.

Centre for Deaf Studies, Trinity College Dublin

Student Name	Student Number		Target Domain	I	II.1	II.2	III	F	%/100
		1	**Target Language - ISL** The TL production is natural and close to an original rendition. It is in line with what is required by the situation (and its function) and the audience (as specified in the translation requirements). We comment on language skill mapped to CEFR: A1-A2 B1-B2 C1-C2	Excellent	Very Good	Good	Borderline	Not satisfactory	
		2	**Functional & Textual Adequacy** The TL accurately accomplishes the goals, purpose (function, information content, expressive demands, persuasive content) set for the intended audience, at the appropriate level of formality.	Excellent	Very Good	Good	Borderline	Not satisfactory	
		3	**Content Meaning** The translation accurately reflects the content of the SL insofar as required without unwarranted alterations, omissions or additions. Slight nuances and shades of meaning are rendered accurately.	Excellent	Very Good	Good	Borderline	Not satisfactory	

Centre for Deaf Studies, Trinity College Dublin

Student Name	Student Number		Target Domain	I	II.1	II.2	III	F	%/100
		1	**Target Language – ENG** The TL production is natural and close to an original rendition. It is in line with what is required by the situation (and its function) and the audience (as specified in the translation requirements). We comment on language skill mapped to CEFR as relevant: A1-A2 B1-B2 C1-C2	Excellent	Very Good	Good	Borderline	Not satisfactory	
		2	**Functional & Textual Adequacy** The TL accurately accomplishes the goals, purpose (function, information content, expressive demands, persuasive content) set for the intended audience, at the appropriate level of formality.	Excellent	Very Good	Good	Borderline	Not satisfactory	
		3	**Content Meaning** The translation accurately reflects the content of the SL insofar as required without unwarranted alterations, omissions or additions. Slight nuances and shades of meaning are rendered accurately.	Excellent	Very Good	Good	Borderline	Not satisfactory	

Centre for Deaf Studies, Trinity College Dublin

DF 4019 Simultaneous Interpreting 2 Exam (90%) (first page)

Student name:

Student Number:

		No	Yes		
				Performance is not reliable enough for professional practice	Emerging – *will need additional supervision and mentoring in professional practice*	Consistently good quality – fit for practice.
1	**Professionalism:** The interpreter is punctual.				
2	**Professionalism:** The interpreter is dressed appropriately for the situation & is mannerly with all parties.				
3	**Preparation:** The interpreter consults with the provider to learn the goals of the interpreted encounter & to assess language requirements				
4	**Practical Issues:** The interpreter positions him/herself so that s/he is seen and heard by both parties.				
5	**Accuracy:** The interpreter can accurately relay the message between clients. The interpreter converts messages expressed in one language into their equivalent in the other, so that the interpreted message can elicit the same response as the original. The interpreter notices his/her own errors and corrects in an unobtrusive manner				
6	**Affect & Flow** – The interaction flows. The clients feel as if they are communicating directly with one another. The interpreter seeks clarification in a culturally appropriate manner as necessary.				
7	**Ethics:** The interpreter behaves ethically throughout the assignment.				
8	**Language Skills:** The interpreter presents the ISL TL message clearly.				
9	**Language Skills:** The interpreter presents the English TL message clearly.				
10	**Interactive Interpreting Skills:** The interpreter negotiates the interaction effectively.				

Centre for Deaf Studies, Trinity College Dublin

DF 4019 Simultaneous Interpreting 2 Exam (90%) (first page)

Student name:

Student Number:

Comments: (Please comment on preparation, processing and product.

Signed (First Marker): Date:

Signed (Second Marker): Date:

Simultaneous Interpreting: British Sign Language to English

	Outstanding / Excellent (100 – 80%)	Very Good (79-70%)	Good (69-60%)	Competent/ Pass (59-40%)	Fail/ Not satisfactory (39-0%)
The overall interpretation: accuracy and effectiveness	The interpretation cannot be improved upon.	The interpretation shows a very high level of accuracy with all main concepts skilfully rendered into the target language.	The interpretation shows a good level of accuracy with all the main concepts effectively rendered into the target language.	Main concepts have been understood and rendered adequately. Some omissions and additions which do not significantly alter the sense of the message.	Inaccuracy in the interpretation. Omissions and additions have been incorporated which significantly alter the sense of the message.
	Outstanding/ excellent comprehension of the source text with virtually no identifiable problems of any kind. The sense is fully conveyed and skilfully articulated with appropriate cultural and linguistic additions.	Very good comprehension of the source text with only minor identifiable problems. The sense is fully conveyed, and very well-articulated with appropriate cultural and linguistic additions.	Good comprehension of the source text with only minor identifiable problems. The sense is conveyed and well-articulated with some appropriate cultural and linguistic additions.	Satisfactory comprehension of the source text.	Limited comprehension of the source text. Main concepts have not been understood and rendered adequately.
	Exceptional awareness of how different social and cultural contexts affect the nature of language and meaning.	Very good awareness of how different social and cultural contexts affect the nature of language and meaning.	Good awareness of how different social and cultural contexts affect the nature of language and meaning.	Some awareness of how different social and cultural contexts affect the nature of language and meaning.	Little/no awareness of how different social and cultural contexts affect the nature of language and meaning.
					The interpretation was unsuccessful.
	Outstanding management of any turn taking issues.	Very good management of any turn taking issues	Good management of any turn taking issues	Turn taking issues are managed competently.	Issues with turn taking are not managed well.
Effective use of Preparation	Evidence of extremely thorough research and preparation of the area/topic.	Evidence of very good research and preparation of the area/topic.	Evidence of a good level of research and preparation of the area/topic.	Adequate level of research/preparation of the area/topic.	Lack of appropriate preparation/ research has led to inaccurate use of language.

BA (Hons.) Interpreting: BSL/English University of Wolverhampton, UK. 2013© Level 6 Master Matrix

Simultaneous Interpreting: British Sign Language to English

	Excellent understanding of the protocols governing the situation. Prior research is used to enhance delivery of the interpretation.	Very good understanding of the protocols governing the situation. Prior research is used to enhance delivery of the interpretation.	A good understanding of the protocols governing the situation. Some prior research is used to enhance delivery of the interpretation.	Evidence of a general understanding of the protocols governing the situation.	Little or no evidence of adherence to/knowledge of the protocols governing the situation. Limited knowledge of the area/topic has led to difficulties in comprehension and delivery.
	The preparatory period with the client is conducted in a highly professional yet personable manner which allows information to be gained which aids the interpretation.	The preparatory period with the client is conducted in a professional yet personable manner which allows information to be gained which aids the interpretation.	The preparatory period with the client is conducted in a reasonably professional manner, demonstrating good interpersonal skills which allows information to be gained to aid the interpretation	The preparatory period with the client is conducted in a professional manner.	Preparatory work is not evident. Lack of interpersonal skills.
Self-control & presentation	Outstanding demonstration of controlled non-verbal behaviour and body language. Impartiality and professionalism is maintained within the performance before, during and after the interpreting assignment.	Very good demonstration of controlled non-verbal behaviour and body language. Impartiality and professionalism maintained within the performance before, during and after the interpreting assignment.	Good demonstration of controlled non-verbal behaviour and body language. Impartiality and professionalism maintained within the performance before, during and after the interpreting assignment.	Some evidence of conscious awareness of personal performance Satisfactory demonstration of controlled non-verbal behaviour and body language. Impartiality and professionalism is maintained within the performance, during and after the interpreting assignment.	Little or no control of verbal or non-verbal behaviour i.e. muttering under breath/swearing/emotional displays/inappropriate excuses for performance or outbursts/exclamations at start/ end of assessment etc.
Register/Style, Mood & Intent	Outstanding/excellent flair for stylistic manipulation of English.	Very good flair for stylistic manipulation of English.	Effective manipulation of English.	Competent manipulation of English.	Little or no evidence of language manipulation.
Pace & Pausing, Management of processing time/	The interpretation sounds as if the signer/speaker was	The interpretation sounds as if the signer/speaker	The interpretation generally sounds as if the	The interpretation mainly sounds as if the	The interpretation sounds awkward and is

BA (Hons.) Interpreting: BSL/English   University of Wolverhampton, UK. 2013©   Level 6 Master Matrix

Simultaneous Interpreting: British Sign Language to English

Criterion	(Outstanding)	(Very Good)	(Good)	(Satisfactory)	(Fail)
prediction and anticipation.	rendering in English as a first language.	was rendering in English as a first language.	signer/speaker was rendering in English as a first language.	signer/speaker was rendering in English as a first language.	generally/entirely literal.
	Outstanding/ excellent ability to maintain consistent stylistic register and to vary it when necessary.	Very good ability to maintain consistent stylistic register and to vary it when necessary.	Good ability with some minor difficulties in maintaining stylistic register.	Variable ability in maintaining stylistic register.	There is clear difficulty in maintaining stylistic register.
	Outstanding/excellent use of time to process information and render the message in the target language.	Very good use of time to process information and render the message in the target language.	Good use of time to process information and render the message in the target language.	Satisfactory use of time to process information and render the message in the target language.	Little or no satisfactory use of time/ coping strategies.
	Exceptional level of ease shown in interpretation/translation, when dealing with a wide range of topics and registers.	Very good level of ease shown in interpretation when dealing with a wide range of topics and registers.	Good level of ease shown in interpretation when dealing with a wide range of topics and registers.	Variable ability shown in interpretation when dealing with a wide range of topics and registers.	Obvious inability to deal with the range of topics and registers within the assignment.
Comprehension: Management of Source knowledge (known/unknown)	Outstanding/excellent comprehension of a wide range of vocabulary and structures. Specialised vocabulary may present some minor problems but there were very clear plausible attempts/strategies to overcome these problems.	Very good comprehension of a wide range of vocabulary and structures. Specialised vocabulary presents some problems but there were clear plausible attempts/strategies to overcome these problems.	Good comprehension of a wide range of vocabulary and structures. Specialised vocabulary presents some problems but there were plausible attempts/strategies to overcome these problems.	Satisfactory comprehension of a wide range of vocabulary and structures. Specialised vocabulary presents some problems but there were some plausible attempts/strategies to overcome these problems.	Comprehension of original is significantly impeded. Specialised vocabulary is not known and is rendered literally or not at all.
Conceptual Rendering/Restructuring	The interpretation demonstrates exceptional knowledge and understanding of the	The interpretation demonstrates very good knowledge and understanding of the	The interpretation demonstrates good knowledge and understanding of the	The interpretation demonstrates some knowledge and understanding of the	The interpretation demonstrates little or no evidence of knowledge and understanding of the

BA (Hons.) Interpreting: BSL/English   University of Wolverhampton, UK. 2013©   Level 6 Master Matrix

Simultaneous Interpreting: British Sign Language to English

	structures, registers and language varieties from the source language. Clear evidence of highly sophisticated restructuring of language throughout the interpretation/translation.	structures, registers and language varieties from the source language. Clear evidence of sophisticated restructuring of language throughout the interpretation/translation.	structures, registers and language varieties from the source language. Evidence of effective restructuring of language throughout the interpretation/translation.	structures, registers and language varieties from the source language. Evidence of effective restructuring of language in the majority of concepts.	structures, registers and language varieties from the source language. Highly literal rendering, which does not reflect source language.
Vocabulary	Outstanding/excellent command of an extensive range of vocabulary and appropriate terminology. Highly sophisticated awareness of the affective power of language (understanding of the lexical choices that are made and why).	Very good command of a broad range of vocabulary and appropriate terminology. Sophisticated awareness of the affective power of language (understanding of the lexical choices that are made and why).	Good command of a broad range of vocabulary and appropriate terminology. Solid awareness of the affective power of language (understanding of the lexical choices that are made and why).	Satisfactory command of a range of lexical choices and generally appropriate terminology. General awareness of the affective power of language (understanding of the lexical choices that are made and why).	Little consideration of lexical choices. Terminology is generally inappropriate or very basic. There is little or no awareness or consideration of the affective power of language and how it impacts on meaning.
Content, Accuracy, Economy & Effectiveness	Content is fully accurate throughout. The interpretation shows detailed understanding and knowledge of subject. Excellent demonstration of clear thinking.	Content is accurate throughout with very minor errors. The interpretation shows very good understanding and knowledge of subject. Very good demonstration of clear thinking.	Content is accurate with minor errors. The interpretation shows good understanding and knowledge of subject. Good demonstration of clear thinking.	Content is accurate with minor errors throughout. The interpretation shows satisfactory understanding and knowledge of subject. Satisfactory demonstration of clear thinking.	The interpretation contains errors which change the meaning of the original. Without knowledge of the source text it is difficult to ascertain the meaning and intent of the original. Confused thinking is evident.
Error Repair/Clarification	There is very clear awareness of errors made, which is shown by subsequent corrections or additions.	There is clear awareness of errors made, which is shown by subsequent corrections or additions.	There is clear awareness of errors made, which is shown by subsequent corrections or additions. Corrections and additions made were mostly	Some awareness of errors made, followed by an attempt to correct/add information. Corrections and additions made, generally clarified	There is little or no awareness of errors made. The majority of mistakes were not rectified. Attempts to correct information resulted in

BA (Hons.) Interpreting: BSL/English University of Wolverhampton, UK. 2013© Level 6 Master Matrix

Simultaneous Interpreting: British Sign Language to English

	Outstanding/ Excellent	Very Good	Good	Partial	Little or no evidence
	Clear evidence of the interpretation being monitored.	Clear evidence of the interpretation being monitored.	Clear evidence of the interpretation being monitored.	the meaning, however a few concepts were still unclear.	further confusion and loss of meaning.
	The audience is informed when a mistake is made.	The audience is informed when a mistake is made.	The audience is informed when a mistake is made.	The audience is generally kept informed when a mistake is made.	The audience is generally not kept informed when a mistake is made.
	Clarification is sought in a culturally appropriate manner.	Clarification is sought in a culturally appropriate manner.	Clarification is sought in a culturally appropriate manner.	Most clarifications are sought appropriately.	The majority of clarifications were not sought appropriately. No clarification was sought even when needed. There were too many attempts to seek clarification resulting in a breakdown of communication.
Interpersonal skills & personal attributes	Outstanding/ Excellent demonstration of: Effective & appropriate communication, presentation, interaction.	Very Good demonstration of: Effective & appropriate communication, presentation, interaction.	Good demonstration of: Effective & appropriate communication, presentation, interaction.	Partial demonstration of: Effective & appropriate communication, presentation, interaction.	Little or no evidence of: Effective & appropriate communication, presentation, interaction.
	The ability to work creatively and flexibly within domain. Mediating skills, qualities of empathy. Self-reliance, taking initiative, adaptability and flexibility.	The ability to work creatively and flexibly within domain. Mediating skills, qualities of empathy. Self-reliance, taking initiative, adaptability and flexibility.	Is able to adapt to the domain. Self-reliance, taking initiative.	Some basic evidence of adaptability but shows reliance on others in the domain rather than using initiative. Appropriate conduct for the setting, shows objectivity within the interpretation.	Inability to be flexible/adaptable. Totally reliant on other participants to take the initiative.

BA (Hons.) Interpreting: BSL/English University of Wolverhampton, UK. 2013© Level 6 Master Matrix

Simultaneous Interpreting: British Sign Language to English

Ability to think and render effectively under pressure. Appropriate conduct for the setting, shows objectivity within the interpretation, overall ability to manage communication dynamic including self-determined positioning & negotiation.	Ability to think and render effectively under pressure. Appropriate conduct for the setting, shows objectivity within the interpretation, overall ability to manage communication dynamic including self-determined positioning & negotiation.	Ability to think and render effectively under pressure. Appropriate conduct for the setting, shows objectivity within the interpretation, overall ability to manage communication dynamic including self-determined positioning & negotiation.	Some attempt made to manage communication dynamic including self-determined positioning & negotiation	Inappropriate conduct for the setting, overall inability to manage communication dynamic including self-determined positioning & negotiation

BA (Hons.) Interpreting: BSL/English   University of Wolverhampton, UK. 2013©   Level 6 Master Matrix

Simultaneous Interpreting: English to British Sign Language

	Outstanding/ Excellent (100 – 80%)	Very Good (79 – 70%)	Good (69 – 60%)	Competent/ Pass (59 – 40%)	Not satisfactory/ Fail (39 – 0%)
The overall interpretation: accuracy and effectiveness	The interpretation cannot be improved upon. Outstanding/ excellent comprehension of the source text with virtually no identifiable problems of any kind. The sense is fully conveyed and skilfully articulated with appropriate cultural and linguistic additions. Exceptional awareness of how different social and cultural contexts affect the nature of language and meaning.	The interpretation shows a very high level of accuracy with all main concepts skilfully rendered into the target language. Very good comprehension of the source text with only minor identifiable problems. The sense is fully conveyed, and very well-articulated with appropriate cultural and linguistic additions. Very good awareness of how different social and cultural contexts affect the nature of language and meaning.	The interpretation shows a good level of accuracy with all main concepts effectively rendered into the target language. Good comprehension of the source text with only minor identifiable problems. The sense is conveyed and well-articulated with some appropriate cultural and linguistic additions. Good awareness of how different social and cultural contexts affect the nature of language and meaning.	Satisfactory comprehension of the source text. Main concepts have been understood and rendered adequately. Some omissions and additions which do not significantly alter the sense of the message. Some awareness of how different social and cultural contexts affect the nature of language and meaning.	The assessor (without seeing the original content) does not immediately understand the signed interpretation. Articulation may be clear but lacks coherence and linkage to enable comprehension to audience/assessor.
Effective use of preparation	Evidence of extremely thorough research and preparation of the area/topic. Excellent understanding of the protocols governing the situation.	Evidence of very good research and preparation of the area/topic. Very good understanding of the protocols governing the situation.	Evidence of a good level of research and preparation of the area/topic. A good understanding of the protocols governing the situation.	Adequate level of research/preparation of the area/topic. Evidence of a general understanding of the protocols governing the situation.	Lack of appropriate preparation/ research has led to inaccurate use of language. Little or no evidence of adherence to/knowledge of the protocols governing the situation.

BA (Hons.) Interpreting: BSL/English University of Wolverhampton, UK. 2013© Level 6 Master Matrix

Simultaneous Interpreting: English to British Sign Language

	Prior research is used to enhance delivery of the interpretation. The preparatory period with the client is conducted in a highly professional yet personable manner which allows information to be gained which aids the interpretation.	Prior research is used to enhance delivery of the interpretation. The preparatory period with the client is conducted in a professional yet personable manner which allows information to be gained which aids the interpretation.	Some prior research is used to enhance delivery of the interpretation. The preparatory period with the client is conducted in a reasonably professional manner, demonstrating good interpersonal skills which allows information to be gained to aid the interpretation	Limited evidence that the interpretation has been enhanced by prior research.	Limited knowledge of the area/topic has led to difficulties in comprehension and delivery. Preparatory work is not evident.
Self-control & presentation	Outstanding demonstration of controlled non-verbal behaviour and body language. Impartiality and professionalism is maintained within the performance before, during and after the interpreting assignment.	Very good demonstration of controlled non-verbal behaviour and body language. Impartiality and professionalism maintained within the performance before, during and after the interpreting assignment.	Good demonstration of controlled non-verbal behaviour and body language. Impartiality and professionalism maintained within the performance before, during and after the interpreting assignment.	Some evidence of conscious awareness of personal performance Satisfactory demonstration of controlled non-verbal behaviour and body language. Impartiality and professionalism is maintained within the performance during and after the interpreting assignment.	Little or no control of verbal or non-verbal behaviour i.e. muttering under breath/swearing/emotional displays/inappropriate excuses for performance or outbursts/exclamations at start/ end of assessment etc.
Reflecting style/mood/intent/register – Style, Character & Mood – Message Emphasis and characteristics demonstrating/ using NMF, signing space, vocabulary, body language.	Outstanding/excellent flair for stylistic manipulation of BSL The BSL interpretation is rendered fluently and confidently in a natural style.	Very good flair for stylistic manipulation of BSL The BSL interpretation is rendered fluently and confidently in a natural style.	Effective manipulation of BSL The BSL interpretation is rendered in a generally fluent and natural style with some confidence.	Confident manipulation of BSL The BSL interpretation is rendered in a mainly fluent and natural style with some confidence.	Little or no evidence of language manipulation. The interpretation looks awkward and is generally/entirely literal.

Level 6 Master Matrix

Simultaneous Interpreting: English to British Sign Language

Criterion	Outstanding/Excellent	Very Good	Good	Satisfactory/Variable	Fail
Intent – the underlying meaning / Processing time and prediction/anticipation	Outstanding/ excellent ability to maintain consistent stylistic register and to vary it when necessary. Excellent BSL style which is exceptionally clear, visual and highly creative. Excellent/outstanding ability to show different characteristics without mocking/excessive mimicry. Outstanding/excellent use of time to process information and render the message in the target language. Exceptional level of ease shown in interpretation when dealing with a wide range of topics and registers.	Very good ability to maintain consistent stylistic register and to vary it when necessary. Highly competent BSL style which is very clear, visual and creative. Evidence of a high level of ability to show different characteristics without mocking/excessive mimicry. Very good use of time to process information and render the message in the target language. High level of ease shown in interpretation when dealing with a wide range of topics and registers.	Good ability to maintain consistent stylistic register with some minor difficulties. BSL style is clear, visual and shows some elements of creativity. Evidence of the ability to show different characteristics without mocking/excessive mimicry. Good use of time to process information and render the message in the target language. Good level of ease shown in interpretation when dealing with a wide range of topics and registers.	Variable ability to maintain stylistic register with some difficulties. BSL style is generally clear, with some visual elements and shows some creativity in the main ideas. An attempt has been made to show different characteristics without mocking/excessive mimicry.	There is clear difficulty in maintaining stylistic register. Some idiosyncratic use of BSL. BSL style does not reflect the source language. Little or no satisfactory use of processing time / coping strategies. Obvious inability to deal with the range of topics and registers within the assignment.
Management of Source language knowledge (known & unknown)	Outstanding/excellent comprehension of a wide range of vocabulary and structures. Specialised vocabulary presents some minor problems but there were very clear plausible	Very good comprehension of a wide range of vocabulary and structures. Specialised vocabulary presents some problems but there were clear plausible	Good comprehension of a wide range of vocabulary and structures. Specialised vocabulary presents some problems but there were plausible attempts/strategies to overcome these	Satisfactory comprehension of a wide range of vocabulary and structures. Specialised vocabulary presents problems but there were some plausible attempts/strategies to	Comprehension of original is significantly impeded. The interpretation demonstrates little or no evidence of knowledge and understanding of the

BA (Hons.) Interpreting: BSL/English   University of Wolverhampton, UK. 2013©   Level 6 Master Matrix

Simultaneous Interpreting: English to British Sign Language

	attempts/strategies to overcome these problems.	attempts/strategies to overcome these problems.	problems.	overcome these problems.	structures, registers and language varieties from the source language.
Conceptual Rendering/Restructuring	The interpretation demonstrates exceptional knowledge and understanding of the structures, registers and language varieties from the source language. Clear evidence of highly sophisticated restructuring of language throughout the interpretation/translation. Highly sophisticated rendering of concepts into the target language.	The interpretation demonstrates very good knowledge and understanding of the structures, registers and language varieties from the source language. Clear evidence of sophisticated restructuring of language throughout the interpretation/translation. Concepts are clearly created and fully completed.	The interpretation translation demonstrates good knowledge and understanding of the structures, registers and language varieties from the source language. Evidence of effective restructuring of language throughout the interpretation/translation. Concepts are generally clear and completed.	The interpretation demonstrates some knowledge and understanding of the structures, registers and language varieties from the source language. Evidence of effective restructuring of language in the majority of concepts. Main concepts are clear and completed, with minor inconsistencies.	Highly literal rendering, which does not reflect source language. Mainly partial or incomplete rendering of concepts.
Vocabulary	Outstanding/excellent command of an extensive range of vocabulary and appropriate terminology, alongside correct and contextual use of signs. Highly sophisticated awareness of the affective power of language (understanding of the lexical choices that are made and why).	Very good command of a broad range of vocabulary and appropriate terminology, alongside correct and contextual use of signs. Very good awareness of the affective power of language (understanding of the lexical choices that are made and why).	Good command of a broad range of vocabulary and appropriate terminology, alongside correct and contextual use of signs. Solid awareness of the affective power of language (understanding of the lexical choices that are made and why).	Satisfactory command of a range of lexical choices and generally appropriate terminology, alongside mostly correct and contextual use of signs. General awareness of the affective power of language (understanding of the lexical choices that are made and why).	Little consideration of lexical choices. Terminology is generally inappropriate. Signs used are incorrectly used or out of context. There is little or no awareness or consideration of the affective power of language and how it impacts on meaning.

BA (Hons.) Interpreting: BSL/English   University of Wolverhampton, UK. 2013©   Level 6 Master Matrix

Simultaneous Interpreting: English to British Sign Language

Content, Accuracy, Economy & Effectiveness	Content is fully accurate throughout. The interpretation shows a detailed understanding and knowledge of subject. Excellent demonstration of clear thinking.	Content is accurate throughout with very minor errors. The interpretation shows a very good understanding and knowledge of subject. Very good demonstration of clear thinking.	Content is accurate with minor errors. The interpretation shows a good understanding and knowledge of subject. Good demonstration of clear thinking.	Content is accurate with minor errors throughout. The interpretation shows a satisfactory understanding and knowledge of subject. Satisfactory demonstration of clear thinking.	The interpretation contains errors which change the meaning of the original. Without knowledge of the source text it is difficult to ascertain the meaning and intent of the original. Confused thinking is evident.
Error Repair/Clarification	There is very clear awareness of errors made, which is shown by subsequent corrections or additions. Clear evidence of the interpretation being monitored. The audience is informed when a mistake is made. Clarification is sought in a culturally appropriate manner	There is clear awareness of errors made, which is shown by subsequent corrections or additions. Clear evidence of the interpretation being monitored. The audience is informed when a mistake is made. Clarification is sought in a culturally appropriate manner	There is clear awareness of errors made, which is shown by subsequent corrections or additions. Corrections and additions made were mostly effective. Clear evidence of the interpretation being monitored. The audience is informed when a mistake is made. Clarification is sought in a culturally appropriate manner	Some awareness of errors made, followed by an attempt to correct/add information. Corrections and additions made, generally clarified the meaning, however a few concepts were still unclear. The audience is generally kept informed when a mistake is made. Most clarifications are sought appropriately.	There is little or no awareness of errors made. The majority of mistakes were not rectified. Attempts to correct information resulted in further confusion and loss of meaning. The audience is generally not kept informed when a mistake is made. The majority of clarifications were not sought appropriately. No clarification was sought even when needed. There were too many attempts to seek clarification resulting in a breakdown of communication.

Simultaneous Interpreting: English to British Sign Language

	Outstanding/ Excellent demonstration of: Effective & appropriate communication, presentation, interaction.	Very Good demonstration of: Effective & appropriate communication, presentation, interaction.	Good demonstration of: Effective & appropriate communication, presentation, interaction.	Partial Demonstration of: Effective & appropriate communication, presentation, interaction.	Little or no evidence of: Effective & appropriate communication, presentation, interaction.
Interpersonal skills & personal attributes	The ability to work creatively and flexibly within domain. Mediating skills, qualities of empathy. Self-reliance, taking initiative, adaptability and flexibility. Ability to think and render effectively under pressure. Appropriate conduct for the setting, shows objectivity within the interpretation, overall ability to manage communication dynamic including self-determined positioning & negotiation and turn-taking.	The ability to work creatively and flexibly within domain. Mediating skills, qualities of empathy. Self-reliance, taking initiative, adaptability and flexibility. Ability to think and render effectively under pressure. Appropriate conduct for the setting, shows objectivity within the interpretation, overall ability to manage communication dynamic including self-determined positioning & negotiation and turn-taking.	Is able to adapt to the domain. Self-reliance, taking initiative. Ability to think and render effectively under pressure. Appropriate conduct for the setting, shows objectivity within the interpretation, overall ability to manage communication dynamic including self-determined positioning & negotiation and turn-taking.	Some basic evidence of adaptability but shows reliance on others in the domain rather than using initiative. Generally appropriate conduct for the setting, showing some objectivity within the interpretation. Some attempt made to manage communication dynamic including self-determined positioning & negotiation and turn-taking.	Inability to be flexible/adaptable. Totally reliant on other participants to take the initiative. Inappropriate conduct for the setting, overall inability to manage communication dynamic including self-determined positioning & negotiation and turn-taking.

BA (Hons.) Interpreting: BSL/English   University of Wolverhampton, UK. 2013©   Level 6 Master Matrix

BSL LANGUAGE MARKING MATRIX

Module............ Assessment............ Name............

	Outstanding/ Excellent 100 – 80%	Very Good 79 – 70%	Good 69 – 60%	Competent/ Pass 59 – 40%	Not satisfactory/ Fail 39 – 0%
Grammar	☐ Excellent use of spatial visual structure ☐ Effective use of Topic/comment structure ☐ Excellent use of lip-patterns ☐ Outstanding linkage of signing	☐ Good use of spatial visual structure ☐ Well established use of Topic/comment structure ☐ Appropriate use of lip-patterns for Nouns/Verb ☐ good linkage of signing	☐ Correct use of spatial visual structure ☐ Topic/comment structure. ☐ Appropriate use of lip-patterns ☐ Shows evidence of clear linkage	☐ Some incorrect use of spatial grammar ☐ Use of Topic/comment structure – development required ☐ Several inappropriate use of lip-patterns ☐ Some clear linkage of your signing	☐ Incorrect use of spatial grammar ☐ None or limited use of Topic/comment structure ☐ Inappropriate/constant use of lip-patterns ☐ Unclear linkage of signing structures
Handshapes	☐ Excellent use of correct handshapes ☐ Iconic orientation correct ☐ Appropriate proform handshape ☐ Concise fingerspelling	☐ Very good use of correct handshapes ☐ Iconic orientation correct ☐ Appropriate proform handshape ☐ Clear fingerspelling	☐ Using correct/some handshapes ☐ Iconic orientation ☐ Appropriate proform handshape ☐ Fingerspelling	☐ Using some incorrect handshapes ☐ Iconic orientation, some were incorrect. ☐ Mainly correct proforms with minor exceptions ☐ Unclear fingerspelling	☐ Using incorrect handshapes. ☐ Iconic orientation, incorrect ☐ Inappropriate proform handshape ☐ Imprecise fingerspelling
N.M.F.	☐ Showing full use of NMF ☐ Sophisticated use of markers ☐ Showing a distinct difference between a question and a response. (Negation & affirmation)	☐ Showing very good use of NMF ☐ Clear evidence of markers ☐ Showing a distinct difference between a question and a response. Negation & affirmation	☐ Showing competent use of NMF ☐ Some evidence of markers ☐ Showing a difference between a question and a response Negation & affirmation	☐ Showing limited use of NMF ☐ Some evidence of markers although this is inconsistent. ☐ Showing a vague distinction between a question and a response	☐ Showing limited or no use of NMF ☐ No evidence of markers ☐ Showing an unclear distinction between a question and a response
Use of spatial grammar	☐ Excellent/Outstanding consistent use of placement ☐ Point of place/person/ Signing space is fully exploited ☐ Excel; Use of eye gaze ☐ Sophisticated reflection of past/present	☐ Well-established and consistent use of placement ☐ Point place/person/ ☐ Appropriate/use signing space. ☐ V good use of eye gaze ☐ Very good reflection in time	☐ Effective use of placement /referencing ☐ Point of place/person ☐ Competent use made of the signing space ☐ Use of eye gaze ☐ Mainly accurate reflection of past/present	☐ Some established use of placement and referencing ☐ Point of place/person/ ☐ Limited use made of the signing space ☐ Some use of eye-gaze. ☐ Reflection of past/present & future was sometimes unclear	☐ Minimal or no established use of placement/references. ☐ Poor point place/person ☐ No use/inappropriate use of the signing space. ☐ Using many incorrect directions for directional verbs ☐ Incorrect usage of timelines
Reflection/ Emotion including roleshift/ roleplay, pace, style	☐ Excellent demonstration emotions/ characteristics in BSL ☐ Excel rep. of strength/weakness/speed or sizes of objects for clarity ☐ excellent use of variation in signing pace ☐ Excellent use of roleshift ☐ Excellent Register variation from formal to informal ☐ Outstanding ability to express empathic responses and demonstrate continued understanding of/engagement with a signer	☐ Very good demonstration emotions characteristics in BSL. ☐ Very effective rep. of strength/weakness/speed or sizes of objects for clarity ☐ Very good use of variation in signing pace ☐ Very good use of roleshift ☐ Good demonstration of Register variation from formal to informal ☐ Very good ability to express empathic responses and demonstrate continued understanding of/engagement with a signer	☐ Very good demonstration emotions/ characteristics in BSL ☐ Very visually correct strength/weakness/speed or objects ☐ Good use of variation in signing pace ☐ Good use of roleshift ☐ Effective demo of Register variation from formal to informal ☐ Competently expresses empathic responses and demonstrate continued understanding of/engagement with a signer	☐ Some variation in emotion/characteristics in BSL ☐ Show visually some correct strength/weakness/speed or size of objects ☐ Some attempt to vary signing pace ☐ Competent use of roleshift ☐ Some attempt at Register variation from formal to informal ☐ Some ability to express empathic responses and demonstrate continued understanding of/engagement with a signer	☐ No evidence emotions/characteristics. ☐ Show visually incorrect strength/weakness/speed or sizes of the object ☐ Signing pace does not vary or was used unsuccessfully ☐ Unclear or confused roleshift ☐ Little or no demonstration of register variation or inappropriate register ☐ Little demonstration of ability to show/or to express empathic responses and demonstrate continued understanding of/engagement with a signer within conversations

BA (Hons) Interpreting: BSL/English: University of Wolverhampton, UK (2013) ©   Level 6 Master Matrix

BSL LANGUAGE MARKING MATRIX

Module............ Assessment............ Name............

Vocabulary	☐ Demonstrates an extensive vocabulary ☐ Uses highly technical/specialist signs to reflect the topic ☐ Use of complex productive lexicon within BSL linguistic constraints ☐ Excel adopts/tolerates new signs and incorporates them into own active vocabulary ☐ Creating signs to reinforce new words productive/established lexicon	☐ Very wide range of vocabulary ☐ Uses highly technical signs to reflect the topic ☐ Use of complex productive lexicon within BSL linguistic constraints ☐ v good adopts/tolerates new signs and incorporates them into own active vocabulary ☐ Creating signs to reinforce new words productive/established lexicon	☐ Good range of vocabulary ☐ Uses appropriate technical signs to reflect the topic ☐ Use of productive lexicon within BSL linguistic constraints ☐ Evid. adopt/tolerate new signs and incorporate them into own active vocabulary ☐ Creating signs to reinforce new words productive/established lexicon	☐ Limited range of vocabulary, ☐ Some technical signs were to reflect the topic ☐ Creates limited productive lexicon within BSL linguistic constraints ☐ Limited adopt/tolerate new signs and not always incorporating them into active vocabulary ☐ Limited use of signs to. Or limited use of productive lexicon	☐ Minimal range of vocabulary, ☐ No use of technical signs to reflect the topic ☐ Productive lexicon does not fall within BSL linguistic constraints ☐ Unable to adopt/tolerate other new signs and incorporate them into active vocabulary ☐ Unable to create signs to reinforce new words and therefore over uses fingerspelling
Interaction	☐ Confidently establishes a good rapport/interaction with participants in conversation ☐ Outstanding use of nmf's/ body posture ☐ Outstanding/excellent interpersonal behaviour & coping strategies	☐ Confidently establishes a good rapport/interaction with participants in conversation ☐ Very Good use of nmf's/ body posture ☐ Very Good interpersonal behaviour & coping strategies	☐ Demonstrates good rapport/interaction with participants in conversation ☐ Good use of nmf's/ body posture ☐ Good interpersonal behaviour & coping strategies	☐ Demonstrates some rapport/interaction with participants in conversation but this is inconsistent ☐ Some inconsistent use of nmf's/ body posture ☐ Reasonable interpersonal behaviour & coping strategies	☐ Demonstrates no rapport/interaction with participants in conversation ☐ Ineffective or no use of nmf's/ body posture ☐ Unsatisfactory interpersonal behaviour & coping strategies
Fluency	☐ Excellent fluency with no hesitation ☐ Clear demonstration of excellent productive and receptive skills (dialogue)	☐ Very good level of fluency with barely any hesitation ☐ Clear demonstration of very good productive and receptive skills (dialogue)	☐ Good level of fluency with minimal hesitation ☐ Demonstrates good productive and receptive skills (dialogue) with minor errors/ miscomprehension	☐ Reasonable fluency but with some hesitation ☐ Demonstrates competent receptive and productive skills with some hesitation/ need for clarification and some errors	☐ Hesitation/lack of fluency ☐ Evidence of a lack of comprehension and inability to respond to questions appropriately
Presentation Skills	☐ Excellent, well-structured with clear introduction and conclusion and clarity throughout ☐ Content appropriate to presentation aims and includes the use of complex/specialist language ☐ Content conveyed with confidence and evidence of understanding and engages the audience's interest	☐ Very well structured with clear introduction and conclusion ☐ Content appropriate to presentation aims and the language is sufficiently complex ☐ Content conveyed with confidence and evidence of understanding and engages the audience's interest	☐ A structured presentation with a recognisable introduction and conclusion. ☐ Content generally appropriate to presentation aims ☐ Content conveyed with some confidence and evidence of understanding and is interesting	☐ Structure generally clear but lacks cohesion in some areas ☐ Some content requires further development for clarity and relevance ☐ Inconsistent expression of ideas with some evidence of understanding.	☐ Little or no evidence of clear structure ☐ Inappropriate or irrelevant content ☐ Little or no evidence of understanding. Lacks confidence
Analysis	An outstanding level of analytical insight. Identifies appropriate strengths and weaknesses and expresses the analysis extremely clearly and succinctly	A very good level of analytical insight. Identifies appropriate strengths and weaknesses and expresses the analysis clearly and succinctly	A good level of analysis. Identifies the main strengths and weaknesses and expresses the analysis well	A competent analysis which identifies some main areas for improvement and areas of strength, but could go further in critically assessing performance	Analysis is not at the desired level. It is not critical enough and does not identify appropriate areas of strength and weakness. Analysis is not expressed clearly and requires further

BA (Hons) Interpreting: BSL/English: University of Wolverhampton, UK (2013) ©

Level 6 Master Matrix

BSL LANGUAGE MARKING MATRIX

Module............ Assessment............ Name..

				Analysis expressed satisfactorily	improvement
General Contents and Concepts	☐ Concepts are exceptionally well thought through and there is evidence of creative thinking ☐ Concepts show linkage with each other, relay full information ☐ Excellent use of pausing to ensure concepts are discrete one from the other	☐ Concepts are very well thought through and are fully completed before moving onto the next ☐ Concepts show linkage with each other, relay full information ☐ Good uses of pausing to ensure concepts are discrete one from the other	☐ Good use of concepts with most concepts being fully completed before moving on to the next ☐ Most concepts show linkage with each other ☐ Some use of pausing to ensure concepts are discrete one from the other	☐ Concepts muddled/overlap with other concepts which causes difficulty in separating new and old concepts ☐ Concepts show incomplete linkage with each other and reflect unclear message ☐ Limited use of pausing to help achieve separation of concepts	☐ Concepts are not clear/ overlap which leads to confusion/miscomprehension ☐ Little or no conceptual linkage or completion of concepts. ☐ Constant stream of information without pausing or separation of concepts creating unclear/muddled & non-comprehension of message

BA (Hons) Interpreting: BSL/English: University of Wolverhampton, UK (2013) © Level 6 Master Matrix

5IG002 Analysis, Translation & Justification (BSL to English)

Text Analysis	Outstanding/ Excellent 100 – 80%	Very Good 79 – 70%	Good 69 – 60%	Competent/ Pass 59% – 40%	Not Satisfactory / Fail 39% - 0%
What /Content	Exceptionally detailed analysis and comprehensive identification of the content of the text with discussion.	Very good detailed analysis and comprehensive identification of the content of the text with discussion.	Good detailed analysis and comprehensive identification of the content of the text with discussion.	Main aspects of the content have been addressed, however further detail is required.	Aspect of 'What' has not been addressed/ minimal information has been presented. Text is not analysed but merely copied and pasted.
Why/Function	Outstanding identification of the purpose of the text, underpinned with evidence from the text. Excellent use of appropriate descriptors/language has been used to describe the purpose. Outstanding/ excellent clarity and analytical considerations.	Very good identification of the purpose of the text, underpinned with evidence from the text. Very good use of appropriate descriptors/language to describe the purpose. Very good clarity and analytical considerations.	Good identification of the purpose of the text, underpinned with evidence from the text. Good use of appropriate descriptors/language to describe the purpose. Mainly clear and analytical considerations.	Some areas have been identified; purpose has been given, however reasons need to be clearer. Satisfactory use of appropriate descriptors/language to describe the purpose. Mainly clear with some analytical considerations.	Very basic identification of the purpose of the text. With minimal/ no reasons to justify.
Who (Author/audience) / Metanotative Qualities	The sender and the receiver of the text have been identified with exceptionally sound reasons and evidence from the text and from research. Highly sophisticated analytical considerations.	The sender and the receiver of the text have been identified with very sound reasons and evidence from the text and from research. Highly sophisticated analytical considerations.	The sender and the receiver of the text have been identified with sound reasons and evidence from the text and from research. Good analytical considerations.	The sender and the receiver of the text have been identified with reasons and evidence from the text and from research. Satisfactory considerations.	Sender and receiver of the text have not been considered/ clearly identified and or information given has not been underpinned by evidence. Minimal or no information/understanding.
Where	Excellent considerations of the aspect of 'Where'. Possibilities have been identified extremely well and backed up by evidence from the text and/or research.	Very good considerations of the aspect of 'Where'. Possibilities have been identified extremely well and backed up by evidence from the text and/or research.	Good considerations of the aspect of 'Where'. Possibilities have been identified and backed up by evidence from the text and/or research.	Good considerations of the aspect of 'Where'. Possibilities has been identified however not always consistent / backed up with evidence	Not a clear understanding of what 'where' refers to, unclear information with little/no research.
How (manner and medium) /Register/Affect	Outstanding/excellent detail provided to identify the 'How' aspect of the text. Tackled exceptionally well with strong underpinning evidence.	Very good detail provided to identify the 'How' aspect of the text. Tackled very well with strong underpinning evidence.	Good detail provided to identify the 'How' aspect of the text. Clearly tackled with good underpinning evidence.	Satisfactory/partial identification of the 'How' aspect of the text. Tackled clearly with underpinning evidence/ some partial evidence.	It is unclear what the how, relates to and how the decision has been made. Information is vague.

BA (Hons.) Interpreting: BSL/English University of Wolverhampton, UK. 2013©
Level 5 Master Matrix 5– Text Analysis / Translation / Justifications

5IG002 Analysis, Translation & Justification (BSL to English)

When/ Context	Highly sophisticated explanation with detailed evidence given, showing examples of clues & research to underpin decisions made.	Sophisticated explanation with detailed evidence given, showing examples of clues & research to underpin decisions made.	Good explanation with evidence given, showing examples of clues & research to underpin decisions made.	Satisfactory explanation with evidence given, showing some examples of clues & research to underpin decisions made.	Little/No evidence given limited/unclear explanation. Little/ no research conducted or attempts to identify the 'when' aspect.
BSL to English Translation					
Layout (adhering to form / style)	Outstanding/ excellent understanding of style/ format. e.g. address, date, salutation, introduction (purpose for writing), main body of issues, salutations.	Very good understanding of style/ format. e.g. address, date, salutation, introduction (purpose for writing), main body of issues, salutations.	Good understanding of style/ format. e.g. address, date, salutation, introduction (purpose for writing), main body of issues, salutations.	Partial understanding of style/ format. (e.g. address, date, salutation, introduction (purpose for writing), main body of issues, salutations).	Very basic in style and format. Layout has not been fully considered. Limited understanding demonstrated.
Translation Accuracy (including multi-layered meaning/ equivalence).	Content is fully accurate throughout. The translation shows exceptional/ detailed understanding and knowledge of subject and inferred meaning. The intent of the ST has been fully rendered in the TT.	Content is accurate throughout with very minor errors. The translation shows very sound understanding and knowledge of subject and inferred meaning. The intent of the ST as been fully rendered in the TT.	Content is accurate with a few minor errors. The translation shows good understanding and knowledge of subject. The intent/inferred meaning of the ST has been rendered in the TT.	Content is accurate with minor errors throughout. The translation shows satisfactory understanding and knowledge of subject. Most of the inferred meaning and intent of the ST has been rendered in the TT.	The majority of key points have not been translated accurately. The translation contains errors which change the meaning of the original. Without knowledge of the source text it is difficult to ascertain the meaning and intent of the original. Inferred meaning has not been clearly rendered into the TT.
	Excellent demonstration of clear thinking/decision making and achieving equivalent effect in meaning (considering cultural encoding and impact via language use).	Very good demonstration of clear thinking/decision making and achieving equivalent effect in meaning (considering cultural encoding and impact via language use).	Good demonstration of clear thinking/decision making and achieving equivalent effect in meaning (considering cultural encoding and impact via language use).	Satisfactory demonstration of clear thinking/decision making and achieving equivalent effect most of the concepts (considering cultural encoding and impact via language use).	Confused thinking is evident, equivalence is not always achieved.

5IG002 Analysis, Translation & Justification (BSL to English)

Language efficiency & economy	The translation demonstrates exceptional knowledge and understanding of the structures, registers and language use in the source language. Clear evidence of highly sophisticated restructuring of language throughout the translation. Outstanding/ excellent use of lexical choices and grammar throughout to represent concepts effectively. Highly sophisticated and economic use (where appropriate) of language to reflect meaning. No obvious language errors – excellent use of spelling, punctuation and grammar.	The translation demonstrates very good knowledge and understanding of the structures, registers and language varieties from the source language. Clear evidence of sophisticated restructuring of language throughout the translation. Very good use of lexical choices and grammar throughout to represent concepts effectively. Sophisticated and economic use (where appropriate) of language to reflect meaning. No obvious language errors – very good use of spelling, punctuation and grammar.	The translation demonstrates good knowledge and understanding of the structures, registers and language varieties from the source language. Evidence of effective restructuring of language throughout the translation. Good use of lexical choices and grammar to represent concepts effectively. Effective/efficient and economic use (where appropriate) of language to reflect meaning. Minor language errors (spelling, punctuation and grammar).	The translation demonstrates some knowledge and understanding of the structures, registers and language varieties from the source language. Evidence of effective restructuring of language in the majority of concepts. Competent/satisfactory use of lexical choices and grammar to represent concepts effectively (not always consistent). Some consideration of effective/efficient and economic use (where appropriate) of language to reflect meaning. Some language errors – (spelling, punctuation and grammar).	The translation demonstrates little or no evidence of knowledge and understanding of the structures, registers and language varieties from the source language. Highly literal rendering, which does not reflect source language. The translation has little/no consideration for efficiency, effectiveness or impact. Some language choices considered but these are not used consistently. Lexical choices require consideration and further attention. Grammatical, punctuation and spelling errors throughout the translation.
Style/ Register	Outstanding/excellent flair for stylistic manipulation of English. The translation reads as though the signer was rendering in English as a first language. Outstanding/ excellent ability to maintain consistent stylistic register and to vary it when necessary. Excellent English style which is very clear and precise and natural.	Very good flair for stylistic manipulation of English. The translation reads as though the signer was rendering in English as a first language. Very good ability to maintain consistent stylistic register and to vary it when necessary. English style is very clear and precise and natural.	Effective manipulation of English. The translation generally reads as though the signer was rendering in English as a first language. Good ability with some minor difficulties in maintaining stylistic register. English style is generally clear and precise and natural.	Competent manipulation of English. The translation mainly reads as though the signer/speaker was rendering in English as a first language. Variable ability in maintaining stylistic register. English style is generally clear with main ideas presented in a natural style.	Little or no evidence of language manipulation. The interpretation/translation appears awkward and is generally/entirely literal. There is clear difficulty in maintaining stylistic register. English style does not reflect the source language.

5IG002 Analysis, Translation & Justification (BSL to English)

	Outstanding/ excellent	Very good	Good	Satisfactory	Little/ no
Concept coherence & cohesion	Outstanding/ excellent restructuring to allow events to be given in chronological order/ to allow for cohesion and coherence/ ease of comprehension.	Very good restructuring to allow events to be given in chronological order/ to allow for cohesion and coherence/ ease of comprehension.	Good restructuring to allow events to be given in chronological order/ to allow for cohesion and coherence/ ease of comprehension.	Satisfactory restructuring to allow events to be given in chronological order/ to allow for cohesion and coherence/ ease of comprehension.	Little/ no evidence of restructuring to allow events to be given in chronological order/ to allow for cohesion and coherence/ ease of comprehension.
Overall Translation	An excellent translation demonstrating a sophisticated level of skill. Outstanding/ excellent comprehension of the source text with virtually no identifiable problems of any kind. The sense is fully conveyed and skilfully expressed with appropriate cultural and linguistic additions. Exceptional awareness of how different social and cultural contexts affect the nature of language and meaning.	The translation shows a very high level of accuracy with all main concepts skilfully rendered into the target language. Very good comprehension of the source text with only minor identifiable problems. The sense is fully conveyed, and very well expressed with appropriate cultural and linguistic additions. Very good awareness of how different social and cultural contexts affect the nature of language and meaning.	The translation shows a good level of accuracy with all main concepts effectively rendered into the target language. Good comprehension of the source text with only minor identifiable problems. The sense is conveyed, and expressed well with some appropriate cultural and linguistic additions. Good awareness of how different social and cultural contexts affect the nature of language and meaning.	Satisfactory comprehension of the source text. Main concepts have been understood and rendered adequately. Some omissions and additions which do not significantly alter the sense of the message. Some awareness of how different social and cultural contexts affect the nature of language and meaning.	Limited comprehension of the source text. Main concepts have not been understood and rendered adequately. Omissions and additions have been incorporated which significantly alter the sense of the message. Little/no awareness of how different social and cultural contexts affect the nature of language and meaning. The interpretation was unsuccessful.

5IG002 Analysis, Translation & Justification (BSL to English)

Justifications				
Justifications	Outstanding/ excellent evidence of understanding of each type of translation device used. Outstanding/excellent use of detailed examples with underpinning evidence. Exceptionally clear discussion to explain strategies and resolutions of translation problems and where possible multiple examples to illustrate the point.	Very good evidence of understanding of each type of translation device used. Very good use of detailed examples with underpinning evidence. Very clear discussion to explain strategies and resolutions of translation problems and where possible multiple examples to illustrate the point.	Evidence of sound understanding of each type of translation device used. Very good use of detailed examples with underpinning evidence. Clear discussion to explain strategies and resolutions of translation problems and where possible multiple examples to illustrate the point.	Evidence of understanding of each type of translation device used. Some detailed examples with underpinning evidence. Clear discussion to explain strategies and resolutions of translation problems and examples used to illustrate the point.	Evidence of a lack of understanding of (some /all) translation devices. Examples are unclear or do not demonstrate the translator's intentions. No detail given/ explanations lack clarity. Justification requirements have not been adhered to.
Evaluation of Target text/ Self analysis	Highly sophisticated reflection on adequacy and acceptability of translation replacement. Comprehensive identification of errors and how they could be corrected. Sophisticated considerations of audience requirements and the impact of decisions made. Excellent and very sound judgements are evident.	Detailed reflection on adequacy and acceptability of translation replacement. Clear identification of errors and how they could be corrected. Extensive considerations of audience requirements and the impact of the decisions made. Very good judgements.	Reflection on adequacy and acceptability of translation replacement. Clear identification of errors and how they could be corrected. Clear considerations of audience requirements and the impact of the decisions made. Good judgements.	Satisfactory reflection on adequacy and acceptability of translation replacement. Clear identification of errors and how they could be corrected. Some clear considerations of audience requirements and the impact of the decisions made. Mainly satisfactory judgements made.	Little of no reflection on adequacy and acceptability of translation replacement. Reflection is very surface level and does not address the issues in a sound manner. Errors made have not been clearly identified or addressed. Audience requirements have not been considered or have been touched on briefly. Further considerations are required as to the impact of decisions made.

BA (Hons.) Interpreting: BSL/English University of Wolverhampton, UK. 2013©

Level 5 Master Matrix 5– Text Analysis / Translation / Justifications

5IG002 Analysis, Translation & Justification (BSL to English)

General Issues

Spelling, Grammar & punctuation	Outstanding/ excellent use of English grammar, spelling and punctuation.	Very good use of English grammar, spelling and punctuation.	Good use of English grammar, spelling and punctuation. Some occasional minor errors.	Competent use of English grammar, spelling and punctuation. Some minor errors.	Language errors are made throughout/ Language errors have resulted in unclear information.
Bibliography and references	Outstanding/ excellent use of relevant theories. Research/Books/journals/ background information and evidence used have been clearly referenced. Outstanding/ Excellent use of Harvard referencing style. No obvious errors in referencing.	Very good use of relevant theories to underpin points made. Research/Books/journals/ background information and evidence used have been clearly referenced. Very good use of Harvard referencing style. No obvious errors in referencing.	Good use of relevant theories to underpin points made. Research/Books/ journals/background information and evidence used have been clearly referenced. Good use of Harvard referencing style. Very few errors in referencing.	Some use of theory to underpin points made. Research/Books/ background information and evidence used have been clearly referenced using Harvard referencing. Some errors in referencing.	Points made have not been underpin or basic underpinning has been used. Clearer evidence of understanding of theories used. Incorrect or unclear or no referencing. Errors throughout/ Harvard system has not been adhered to.

Basic BSL I Marking Matrix

Student Name: _____

BSL Features	Outstanding/ Excellent 100 – 80%	Very Good 79 – 70%	Good 69 – 60%	Competent/ Pass 59 – 40%	Not satisfactory/ Fail 39% - 0%
Grammar	Outstanding or excellent use of basic syntactic spatial field. Placement very clearly established throughout and use of referencing is evident. Outstanding use of verbs with signs incorporating agreement for subject/object, place, manner and number. Overall outstanding/excellent use of basic grammar.	Very good use of basic syntactic spatial field. Placement is clearly established and use of referencing is evident. Very good use of verbs with signs incorporating agreement for subject/object, place, manner and number. Overall very good use of basic grammar.	Good use of basic syntactic spatial field. Placement is established and use of referencing is evident. Some very minor errors. Good use of verbs with signs incorporating agreement for subject/object, place, manner and number with few errors. Overall good use of basic grammar.	Some use of basic syntactic spatial field, but not consistent. Placement is established and use of referencing is evident. Satisfactory use of verbs with signs incorporating agreement for subject/object, place, manner and number.	No established use of placement/references. Verb signs do not incorporate agreement for subject/object, place, manner and number. Basic grammar use is unclear.
Hand-shapes	Outstanding/ excellent use of hand-shapes with very clear and firm movement and orientations. Classifiers are correct and appropriate. Fingerspelling is very clear and well-paced.	Very good use of hand-shapes with very clear and firm movement and orientations. Classifiers are correct and appropriate. Fingerspelling is very clear and well-paced.	Good use of hand-shapes with clear movement and orientations. Classifiers are correct and appropriate. Fingerspelling is clear and well-paced with some very minor errors.	Competent use of hand-shapes with clear movement and orientations. Classifiers are generally correct and appropriate. Fingerspelling is generally clear and well-paced; however there are a few incorrect spellings and some hesitancy.	There are many unclear and incorrect hand-shapes which impede clarity of the signs. Many incorrect classifiers with incorrect/ unclear movement and orientations. Fingerspelling is hesitant and/or inaccurate throughout.
Non-Manual Features	Outstanding/ excellent use of non-manual features to show basic emotion, questions and general intonation.	Very good use of non-manual features to show basic emotion, questions and general intonation.	Good use of non-manual features to show basic emotion, questions and general intonation.	Some use of non-manual features to show basic emotion, questions and general intonation.	No use of non-manual features to show emotion, questions and general intonation.
Vocabulary	Outstanding/excellent range of vocabulary without being repetitive	Very good range of vocabulary without being repetitive.	Good range of vocabulary without being repetitive	Limited range of vocabulary with some repetition.	- Minimal range of vocabulary with constant repetition.
Interaction	Outstanding/ excellent interaction with participants in conversation. Outstanding/ excellent eye contact maintained throughout. Outstanding/ excellent comprehension.	Very good interaction with participants in conversation. Very good eye contact maintained throughout. Very good comprehension minor clarification needed.	Good interaction with participants in conversation. Good eye contact maintained throughout. Good comprehension some clarification needed and sought.	Satisfactory interaction with participants in conversation. Competent use of eye contact throughout. Fair comprehension with some clarification.	Minimal interaction with participants in conversation. Minimal/no eye contact maintained. Minimal comprehension with constant clarification necessary.
Fluency	Outstanding/ excellent fluency	Very good fluency with little hesitation	Good fluency with some occasional hesitation	Reasonable fluency with some hesitation	Hesitation and a lack of fluency throughout.

BA (Hons.) Interpreting: BSL/English   University of Wolverhampton, UK. 2013©   Level 3 Master Matrix

Basic BSL I Marking Matrix

Student Name: _____

Overall Comments:

Lecturer(s) Name(s): _____   Signature(s): _____

Date: _____   Grade: _____

BA (Hons.) Interpreting: BSL/English   University of Wolverhampton, UK. 2013©   Level 3 Master Matrix

www.ingramcontent.com/pod-product-compliance
Lightning Source LLC
Chambersburg PA
CBHW080438230426
43662CB00015B/2314